P9-CPV-685

"Every [dual-career] couple struggles with how to make a fulfilling life work for both partners. Now, Jennifer Petriglieri has written a book with helpful, real-life stories and practical solutions that actually work! I wish I'd had this book at the beginning and middle of my career. I'm glad to have it in my hands now."

—**JOANNA BARSH,** Director Emerita, McKinsey & Company; coauthor, *How Remarkable Women Lead*

"*Couples That Work* is a sweet, captivating journey into the lives, loves, and lessons of over a hundred couples. An inspiring read for anyone looking to both work and love."

—**LASZLO BOCK,** cofounder and CEO, Humu; former Senior Vice President of People Operations, Google; and author, *Work Rules!*

"In this provocative and thoughtful book, Professor Petriglieri has created a brilliant conversational road map for everyone navigating a dual-career path. I read it with my partner—and suggest you do the same. Fascinating!"

—**LYNDA GRATTON,** Professor of Management Practice, London Business School; coauthor, *The 100-Year Life*

Couples
That Work

Couples That Work

HOW DUAL-CAREER COUPLES CAN THRIVE IN LOVE AND WORK

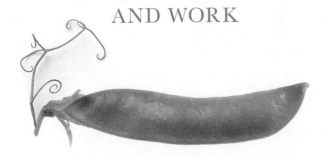

Jennifer Petriglieri

HARVARD BUSINESS REVIEW PRESS

BOSTON, MASSACHUSETTS

HBR Press Quantity Sales Discounts

Harvard Business Review Press titles are available at significant quantity discounts when purchased in bulk for client gifts, sales promotions, and premiums. Special editions, including books with corporate logos, customized covers, and letters from the company or CEO printed in the front matter, as well as excerpts of existing books, can also be created in large quantities for special needs.

For details and discount information for both print and ebook formats, contact booksales@harvardbusiness.org, tel. 800-988-0886, or www.hbr.org/bulksales.

Copyright 2019 Jennifer Petriglieri
All rights reserved
Printed in the United States of America

10 9 8 7 6 5 4 3 2 1

No part of this publication may be reproduced, stored in or introduced into a retrieval system, or transmitted, in any form, or by any means (electronic, mechanical, photocopying, recording, or otherwise), without the prior permission of the publisher. Requests for permission should be directed to permissions@harvardbusiness.org, or mailed to Permissions, Harvard Business School Publishing, 60 Harvard Way, Boston, Massachusetts 02163.

The web addresses referenced in this book were live and correct at the time of the book's publication but may be subject to change.

Library of Congress Cataloging-in-Publication Data

Names: Petriglieri, Jennifer, author.
Title: Couples that work : how dual-career couples can thrive in love and work / Jennifer Petriglieri.
Description: Boston, MA : Harvard Business Review Press, [2019].
Identifiers: LCCN 2019016417 | ISBN 9781633697249 (hardcover)
Subjects: LCSH: Dual-career families. | Work-life balance. | Couples—Psychology. | Work and family. | Quality of life.
Classification: LCC HD4904.25 .P467 2019 | DDC 306.3/6—dc23
LC record available at https://lccn.loc.gov/2019016417

ISBN: 978-1-63369-724-9
eISBN: 978-1-63369-725-6

The paper used in this publication meets the requirements of the American National Standard for Permanence of Paper for Publications and Documents in Libraries and Archives Z39.48-1992.

To Gianpiero, my inspiration and muse.
And to Pietro and Arianna, who fill our life with
joy and surprises.

CONTENTS

Couples
That Work

1

The Three Transitions of a Dual-Career Couple

As Cheryl lay in her hospital bed beside her newborn baby, she couldn't have been happier. She had saved enough to take a three-month unpaid maternity leave from her job in a financial services firm and was relishing the thought of spending long days learning to be a mom to little Annabel. It meant a lot to her. Throughout her childhood, Cheryl had often had to worry about money, and as a young adult, she had worked hard to make sure that her own children would not have to. Her dream was coming true, and she was proud of it. She was a bit nervous, too, about the bigger apartment that she and Mark had bought—they had stretched their budget to make it possible—but she was grateful that Mark's salary would help cover their expenses while she was on leave.

Cheryl was suddenly distracted from her reverie when Mark bounded into the room, his face beaming, bearing the bag of baby clothes they had forgotten in their dash to the hospital. For the past two years, he had put up with a corporate job he hated while networking like mad to move into the startup world. The move had proved elusive, but the birth of Annabel had clearly improved his mood.

Mark kissed Cheryl and picked Annabel up, staring into her eyes as she yawned. "I told you they would be just like yours," he said, then blurted out, "Guess what?" He seemed giddy with excitement.

"What?" replied Cheryl expectantly.

"I just got a call from Sebastien. He secured the first round of funding for his startup, and wants me to join it!"

The blood drained from Cheryl's face. This was exactly the kind of move that Mark had dreamed of, but joining an early-stage startup would mean a huge drop in salary—maybe no salary at all. Their scanty savings and their new mortgage meant that Cheryl would have to go back to work after just a few weeks. Trying to be supportive, she said, "That's so great! Let's talk about the timing once we get home."

"We can't, darling, I'm sorry, Sebastien is moving fast and the time is now," Mark answered, squeezing Cheryl's hand. "I've already resigned. I start there on Monday!"

———

Cheryl and Mark are real people; I have only changed their names. They are one of many couples I spoke to in researching this book. Their story—which we'll come back to in chapter 2—highlights a common theme I heard: so often, for dual-career couples, carefully plotted plans are upended by unexpected events, and the happiest moments in life overlap with sudden changes and challenges. The greatest opportunities spark the toughest, and most revealing, conversations. The most meaningful personal decisions seem to coincide with the most consequential professional opportunities.

While the challenges dual-career couples face are fairly well known, there is a surprising lack of meaningful guidance available on how to deal with them. Most career advice is targeted at individuals, treating major career decisions as if we're flying solo—without partners, children, siblings, friends, or aging parents to consider.

Moreover, most advice for couples focuses on their personal relationship, not the way it intersects with professional dreams. Even then, couples are bombarded with blanket prescriptions on what they should do: "Divide the housework equally," "Strike a balance between life and career," "Make time for one another"— none of which have helped couples become clearer about, let alone learn how to satisfy, their deepest needs in work and in love. Some even label those who strive for fulfillment in both work and love as hopelessly naive.

I believe most current advice has failed couples because it targets surface-level, practical issues, rather than the underlying forces that create those issues. It tells us how we should prioritize our careers, divide housework, and maintain a healthy relationship, rather than exploring why we are struggling with these things in the first place.

Many of the people I spoken to had devised intricate ways to synch their calendars, divide up household responsibilities, and balance their careers. Yet they rarely had a conversation about deeper psychological and social forces, by which I mean their struggles for power and control, the roles they expected each other to play in their shared lives, their personal hopes and fears, and the collective expectations of what defines a good relationship and career that exert a powerful influence on them.

While couples may not talk much about them, these deeper psychological and social forces influence the way they relate and decisions they make. They push and pull on people's behavior and on the shape of their relationship. At times, such as during the transitions this book focuses on, these forces can seem over-whelming and inescapable; at others, they are just a gentle stream that carries couples along. People can be very aware of some of these forces, but others remain implicit or even unconscious. Through my research, I found that if couples don't address them, those forces can hold them back and lead them down a path of conflict. If couples understand and work with them, however, they can ease their practical challenges and help them thrive.

Beyond Dividing the Chores

My aim in writing this book is to move beyond the practicalities and provide a greater understanding of the psychological and social forces underlying the challenges that dual-career couples face. I also show how thinking and talking about these forces can help couples be more successful and fulfilled in love and work.

Five years ago, I set out to lift the lid on the lives of dual-career couples, to understand not just when and why couples struggle, but also when and why couples thrive. And to develop, based on this understanding, a more nuanced approach to guiding couples on how to make their lives work for them.

I started my research with a simple question: *How can dual-career couples thrive in their love and work?* At the beginning of my inquiry, I naively assumed that couples struggled early in their relationships, then at some point figured out how to fit their love and work together in a way that let them travel through their lives more or less smoothly. The further I got into the research, the more clouded the picture became. There were struggles throughout couples' working lives, which meant that they had to revisit how their relationship and careers fit together more than once.

As I interviewed more couples, the fog began to lift. I noticed similarities between their struggles. Moreover, I saw that these struggles were predictable across a couple's life together. I discovered that dual-career couples faced three transitions during their working lives. Each required couples to face different challenges, and each, if well navigated, renewed their relationship and took it to a deeper level.

Mapping out these transitions helped me to understand the challenges that dual-career couples face in a new way. It revealed the psychological and social forces that drove the challenges—life events, conformity pressures, role changes. It also taught me how thinking and talking about these forces can help couples thrive in love and work, avoiding regrets, imbalance, and slowly drifting apart.

The result is this book: a portrait of what dual-career couples' lives are *really* like—and a guide to making them better.

The Rise of Dual-Career Couples

Before we dig in, it is important to recognize that being in a dual-career couple relationship is now the norm. In more than 65 percent of couples in North America and Europe, both partners work, a number that grows each year.[1] Even in countries like Japan, where the proportion of dual-career couples is lower, the trend is consistently upward.[2]

One obvious reason for this trend is economics. In today's expensive and uncertain world, having two salaries helps couples cope with the ever-increasing cost of living and provides a financial safety net should one partner be laid off.

But economic necessity is only part of the picture. Across the globe, couples are becoming more egalitarian. Men and women increasingly define a meaningful life as having a good career *and* having active roles at home. And although it is less often talked about, there is mounting evidence that couples reap benefits when both partners work *and* dedicate themselves to home life.

When one partner has a stable income, the other has more freedom to retrain, explore alternative paths, and make career changes. Taking the plunge to become an entrepreneur, for example, is much more palatable when you know your partner's salary will cover the bills. Research also shows that when both partners work, they have a greater respect for each other's careers, which leads them to feel closer emotionally.[3]

At home, when both partners are active, their children and their relationship benefit. Kids have better social skills and higher academic results when both their parents play with them and help out with homework and when the family eats together.[4] Couples have less conflict, more satisfying relationships, and more sex when both partners contribute substantially to household chores.[5] Perhaps most striking of all, couples in which partners earn roughly the same amount and share the housework equally have a staggering 48 percent lower chance of divorce than the average couple.[6]

Despite this array of benefits, life is not a bed of roses for dual-career couples. Logistics, which are perhaps more straightforward when one partner earns the bread and the other takes care of the home, can be a minefield. Many couples I spoke to shared horror stories of business-travel disasters or sick children on the day when both had critical meetings. Managing life is made even more challenging for those couples who live away from extended families. With smaller social support networks, some couples are under pressure to manage complex personal and family lives alone.

On top of this, careers are more mobile for everyone, in couples or not. Average workers will transition between ten and fifteen organizations over their working life.[7] Organizations no longer guarantee lifetime employment, and people actively move around to pursue growth and opportunities. There are many upsides to having more career choices, but there is no doubt that making these decisions is stressful and can be more so when you're coordinating your choices with those of your beloved.

Even as people place less emphasis on organizational belonging, they place more emphasis on their careers as a source of meaning in their lives. Now more than ever, what we do is intricately connected to who we are and how we define ourselves.[8] With identity, self-esteem, and sense of meaning all wrapped up in our careers, it is no wonder that we are heavily invested in making them successful. In short, we work a lot.

The above trends present dual-career couples with a host of struggles, dilemmas, and questions: Can we both have equally important careers, or must we prioritize one over the other? How can we juggle children and family commitments without sacrificing our work? Does everything require trade-offs, or can we find solutions that benefit us both? And most fundamentally: *How can we thrive in love and in work?*

These questions are not just a matter of academic interest to me. They are questions I have personally lived through and wrestled with for the past fourteen years.

Researching Two-Career Couples While Being Half of One

I decided to quit my career at 3 a.m. one March morning in 2010. I was in the midst of a transition from the corporate to the academic world and, at thirty-three, one of the oldest students on my PhD program. I was also the mother of two wonderful, lively, and extremely wakeful children under two.

Like many new parents, my husband Gianpiero and I were on a roller coaster. We adored the two little creatures we had brought into this world; they gave us a sense of deep meaning and a daily dose of surprises. To us, they were gorgeous in every way; yet the energy and time we needed and wanted to pour into them was often overwhelming. We were on our nineteenth month of interrupted sleep, and the pattern of three or four nightly get-ups showed no sign of abating. We were beyond exhaustion.

As I looked to the coming years, I could not see how we could make it work. We were both ambitious and we had faith in each other's talent, but academia is a demanding, high-pressure, up-or-out system. It's a grind. If Gianpiero did not keep excelling in his teaching and writing, he would lose his job in the business school in which he worked. Likewise, if I did not produce novel, publishable research, I would never find a job. Although we were driven, neither of us was willing to give up too much time with our children or each other. Something had to give.

My friends and parents (who were a dual-career couple themselves) all encouraged me to take time out. Initially, I resisted. I knew that if I stopped for more than a few months, my door to academia would likely close, and I wanted a shot at my dream. I searched for books, advice—anything that could show me a way—but all I found were prescriptions of how to split housework or tales of couples who had somehow found a perfect balance. Gianpiero did a good chunk of the shopping, cooking, and cleaning, but balance eluded us. When 3 a.m. that March morning rolled in, I had had enough. I waited for our breakfast of thick black coffee and warm milk to announce my intentions. I expected his relief and half-hearted resistance. What I got was different.

"That's your sleep deprivation talking," Gianpiero told me. "There is no way I am letting you give your dream up, not now." I sat in stunned silence as he told me that I was about to make a huge mistake that I would bitterly regret, and that he would not stand by and watch me do it. He reminded me that he had been the first person to whom I had confided my wish to do a PhD, and how much it meant to me. He reminded me that this was not the first time I had hesitated since starting, and it would not be the last. I was annoyed. He could tell. I had been looking for tea and sympathy; what I got was a loving kick. Yet he was right. If he had not pushed me to step up and plow through that painful period, there is no way my career would be where it is today. I may not have even had a career.

Gianpiero's loving challenge saved me—or maybe, more precisely, shaped me. He continues to affect who I am not only as a wife and mother, but also as a professional. And I shape him in turn. Hard as it was to take back then, his challenge was not unfamiliar. I had done the very same to him, over another breakfast, a few years before. We were in Sicily, visiting his hometown, and even the excitement of our still-new love could not quench his professional restlessness. He was freelancing as a consultant and instructor, but longed for a full-time teaching job. He had been looking for two years without success, and each rejected application hurt.

That morning, he told me in passing as we ate the local breakfast of almond-flavored granita, he had deleted an email from the department chair of a European business school he would have loved to work at. They had invited him for interviews twice already, but each time, no offer had followed. Now, she had written, there was an opening for an instructor, but only on a temporary basis. He had had enough of gigs and of rejections, he said, and could not take one more.

"You're crazy not to accept. They won't be able to let go of you, once they have you around," I said, knowing something about it.

"You're in love," he replied, "they're in business."

I did not know then that I would end up writing a book about how blurry that line is for dual-career couples, but I could not help replying, "I'm in both." Then I pulled out his laptop, went into his trash email folder, and wrote a one-line reply to his future department chair (and later mine). "When do I start?" He has worked there for thirteen years.

As I put the finishing touches on this book, I know that right now, things are good. I also know that, just as in March 2010, or December 2004, everything in life is a phase. We have faced, and are certain to continue to face, many challenges in our life together. At times, we work through them well; at others, less so. Each time we face a hurdle, I have searched for meaningful advice and mostly come away empty-handed. We, and many of our friends, colleagues, and students, have muddled through our dual-career challenges, not always successfully. Living through my own experiences, and witnessing those of so many others, I have often thought, "There must be a way. There must be a way of approaching this life we have chosen that can help more couples thrive."

Observing Early Patterns

I've spoken to over a hundred couples in the course of my research. Although each couple's story was unique in its details, they experienced similar patterns of highs and lows. All struggled through similar challenges, which they faced at similar periods in their lives and relationships. When I began to see how these patterns cut across couples, and when I realized that the periods of upheaval aligned with career stage and the length of their relationships, I began to think of couples in terms of their life cycles.

It struck me that while psychologists had mapped adults' life cycles, the same had not been done for couples. Neither had anyone mapped how these life stages related to careers, and how people's movement through each stage influences their partner's.

The notion that life is a journey in distinct stages is old. It appears in ancient scriptures, in Shakespeare's plays, and in the work of other great writers. In more recent times, the work of psychologists Erik Erikson and Daniel Levison has led to a deep understanding of adults' life stages and in particular of the transitions between them. In these transitions, Erikson argued, we must resolve developmental issues distinct to each stage.[9] These "crises of development" as Levinson called them, are not only necessary but desirable.[10] It is the developmental crises we face in our transitions that hold the potential for growth, and without them our development stalls.

The deeper I got into my data, the more clearly I saw parallels between the individual developmental transitions that Erikson and Levinson described and those of the couples I studied. I also saw key differences: distinct *couple* transitions and challenges that needed to be addressed for both partners to thrive in the next stage of their relationship, career, and lives.

The Three Transitions

I found that dual-career couples pass through three distinct transitions on their route from becoming a couple to retirement. Each transition plunges a couple into a landscape of new questions, different concerns, and novel ways of relating. And each requires couples to tackle specific psychological and social forces that underpin their relationship. While the transitions push couples to tackle a deeper layer of their relationship and lives, they involve revisiting the agreements forged during previous transitions.

The first transition requires couples to move from having parallel, independent careers and lives to having interdependent ones. The work of this transition is a deliberate accommodation to the first major life event—often a big career opportunity or the arrival of a child—that couples face together. To navigate their first transition, couples must negotiate how to prioritize their careers and divide family commitments in a way that lets them both thrive with few regrets. In doing so, they craft a joint path along which they travel until their second transition.

The work of the second transition is *reciprocal individuation*. Don't be put off by the term. It means that couples must shift their focus from conforming to others' demands and expectations and figure out what they each really want out of their careers, lives, and relationship. This transition is usually sparked by feelings of restlessness and oppression that give way to existential questions of direction and purpose. It requires couples to figure out their unique interests and desires, and renegotiate the roles they play in each other's lives. In doing this work on deeper levels of their relationship, couples also renegotiate the division of career and family labor that they established in their first transition. If completed successfully, the result of this transition is a broader path along which couples travel until they reach their third transition.

Couples' work in the third transition is to reinvent themselves in a way that is grounded in their past accomplishments, while opening possibilities for the future. This transition is triggered by role shifts—becoming the most experienced workers, the empty-nester parents, and being seen as the older generation—that result in identity voids. Those voids come with feelings of loss that must be tended to, but they also make space for new opportunities. Couples can sink into these voids and drift, or they can use them as a place of exploration and reinvention. To do the latter, couples must tackle any unresolved developmental tasks of the first two journeys, then play with the idea of who they might become given their new ambitions and priorities. In doing so, couples craft a path along which they can travel with renewed purpose.

The three transitions are linked. In the first transition, while making deliberate accommodations to a major life event, couples implicitly negotiate the roles they will take in each other's lives. Over time, these roles become constraining and spark the restlessness and questioning that lead to the second transition. The second transition is thus in part about tackling the side effects of the first one. Likewise, the third transition cannot be completed unless couples address regrets and developmental asymmetries left over from their first two transitions.

Some people will face the three transitions with the same partner, while others will move through different transitions with different partners. Despite these variations, all of which I will explore in the book, the three transitions follow a similar pattern.

The Pattern of Transitions

Each transition begins with a trigger that makes it difficult for couples to continue traveling along the path they crafted in their previous stage—be that the independent paths that partners travel on before their first transition, the joint path that couples design in their first transition and travel until their second, or the broadened joint path that couples structure during their second transition and travel until their third.

The triggers for the first transition are major life events that originate from people's careers or personal lives, such as the need to move geographically, a promotion or a layoff, the arrival of a new baby, the need to care for aging parents, or family health issues. The triggers for the second transition originate from our inner worlds and present themselves as existential questions and doubts about whose life we are really living. The third-transition triggers come in the form of role shifts that create identity voids and open up the questions of what to do with the time and energy we have left.

Although the triggers are important, they don't define each transition. The triggers only reveal a transition's defining question. Answering this question becomes the couple's task for each transition. The pattern my research uncovered suggests that the three questions most couples will wrestle with during their transitions are:

- First transition: *How can we make this work?*

- Second transition: *What do we really want?*

- Third transition: *Who are we now?*

These defining questions go to the core of how couples live their lives and how they structure a path to allow both partners to thrive. When couples encounter the defining question of their transition, they are thrown off balance and doubts abound. This destabilization, while unsettling, is actually helpful. It creates the motivation for couples to revisit and recraft their path.

The central experience of all transitions is a period of struggle, when couples are suspended between old and new. They sense that the path they previously traveled on no longer works for them, but are not yet clear how to recraft it. Each transition has a set of traps, unique to its struggle, in which couples can get stuck. Some couples cannot escape these traps, and they end their journey together. Others find direction and figure out how to reshape their path in order to move forward.

After each transition in which they work on their path, couples enter a more stable period in which they travel along it. During these periods, couples relax and enjoy some breathing space. The deeper psychological and social forces that felt all-powerful during their transition recede to being gentle influencers. They build happy memory banks full of special family times, romantic moments, career growth, and activities with friends. Or they just go through familiar routines, enjoying their quiet familiarity. Eventually, they face new triggers and embark on their next transition—and the cycle repeats.

Life Is a Series of Transitions

Although my research revealed that these transitions are predictable, they often come as a surprise to couples. That's what happened to David and Melissa.

They'd just completed a five-hour drive to their Florida home from Emory University in Atlanta, where they had dropped off their youngest child at college. As they settled with a sigh into their usual seats in the kitchen and poured a couple of glasses of their favorite wine, they reflected on the journey that had brought them here.

Thirty years ago, they'd been the ones graduating from college—David, a business major embarking on a promising career at a large accounting firm; Melissa, a psychology major taking her first steps into the world of public relations. They'd married, bought a home in Boston close to their parents, and begun planning a family of their own.

Two lively daughters arrived just eighteen months apart, and life suddenly got complicated: they abruptly found themselves in the first transition, battling sleepless nights while struggling to master increasingly interesting—and difficult—assignments at work. Just as they began to find a rhythm, David was offered a promotion to head a team in Florida.

Their careers had always been on equal footing, but if they moved to Florida, David's would unquestionably take priority. Juggling careers and family had been hard even with parental support nearby; how would they manage over eleven hundred miles away? And what would happen to Melissa's career?

Weeks of agonizing ended with the decision to move south. David's firm helped Melissa find a new job, and his new higher salary helped pay for child care. Their toddlers grew into girls. Weekends exploring Florida beaches, holidays with family, blossoming careers—it was a golden age until the next impasse hit, twelve years later.

Their second transition began in their early forties. David had become disillusioned with corporate life and begun to question whether accounting was still for him. Melissa was longing to strike out on her own. She dreamed of launching her own communications advice agency. But could they afford to explore new options? With two teenagers, a mortgage, and college fees on the horizon, a lot was at stake.

The uncertainty of this phase took a heavy toll on their relationship. Neither David nor Melissa felt that the other truly understood or appreciated their desire for change, and their career dissatisfaction spilled over into their marriage. Petty disagreements fueled growing resentments, and thoughts of divorce crossed their minds more than once. But six years later, they seemed to be back on track. They had supported each other's move to new roles. David had moved into a management position at a smaller accounting firm, where he was enjoying more independence. Melissa had taken the plunge into independent work and, after initially struggling to attract clients, was now thriving. Their girls were happy and excited about college life. David and Melissa felt they'd cracked the dual-career code and become strong role models for their daughters.

So why did they suddenly feel so unsettled? The two sat for a while without speaking, savoring the wine and noticing the unaccustomed quiet in their now-empty house. The little time they had spent just with each other over the past decade was apparent. They were a little awkward, like long-lost friends who, upon being reunited, wonder how much the other has changed. Finally, David broke the silence. He turned to Melissa and admitted, "Honey, I'm just not sure who we are anymore."

Suddenly, after all that they had been through together, they found themselves in a new transition: the third transition.

Many couples I spoke to during the course of my research were surprised by their need to go through successive transitions. Melissa and David had successfully navigated their first two, only to be shocked by the realization that they were now embarking on a third, with an outcome that they could scarcely anticipate. While these transitions can feel arduous, they are also reinvigorating if approached in the right way. They represent a developmental imperative, and they hold the power to give meaning and energy to the lives of dual-career couples, helping them thrive in love and work.

How to Use This Book

The rest of this book is divided into three parts, one for each transition. Every part has three chapters: the first focuses on the triggers of that transition and the developmental question that defines it; the second tackles the transition's struggle period and the traps and dead-ends that can ensnare couples; the third explores how couples can resolve the defining question of that transition and recraft their path. At the end of each part, you'll find a summary of the key dynamics of that transition that you can use to reference back to the exercises and tools in each chapter.

Each chapter begins with the stories of real couples that illustrate that chapter's themes. Throughout the book, I'll share the stories of more than thirty couples I interviewed. You don't need to keep track of all the characters or plotlines. Each story stands on its own, and together they are meant to add richness and variety to the theory and advice, to bring the concepts in this book to life. Each chapter ends with practical ideas and exercises that can help you work through your transition with your partner.

I have written this book for people at all stages of their dual-career life, from recent couples who are at the beginning of their careers to those who are approaching retirement and may be on their second or third significant partnership. Some people will enjoy reading the book from cover to cover. Others will want to dive into the chapters that relate to the transition they are currently in. If you are drawn to the latter approach, I still encourage you to dip into the transition that comes before and after where you currently are. Looking back is a great way of helping you make sense of where you are today, and looking forward can help you anticipate what is to come.

The Research

In all, I collected the stories of 113 couples. The full study design is described in the appendix. The couples whose stories I will chronicle are diverse. They range from high-powered executives occupying C-suites, to midlevel professionals struggling to build their careers, to entrepreneurs laboring to build brand-new companies, to freelancers. They include couples in their early twenties, couples in their sixties, and couples in every decade in between. Some couples are in their first relationship, others in their second, or even third, marriages with complex family situations. They come from thirty-two countries on four continents. Many have children, others are childless; some are straight, others are gay. Their ethnic, religious, and national backgrounds are varied. They all have undergraduate degrees; some have graduate degrees. The commonality among them is that that both partners are committed to their careers and to each other.

In all the couples I spoke to, both partners had *careers*, not just jobs. I follow in the footsteps of much research on careers in defining careers as sequences of professional or managerial jobs that demand a high degree of commitment and have some form of continuous development. Some people with careers hope to reach the top of organizations, but not all. The commonality among them is the central role that work plays in their life, and their commitment to growing in and through their work—be that by moving up a hierarchy, deepening their expertise, or continuing their learning.

I'm sometimes asked why I focused on dual-career couples, and not on all couples in which both partners work. The reason is that for people who have a career orientation, work is a central piece of their identity. Their psychological investment in and commitment to their work sits alongside their commitment to their relationship. It is this combination of commitments that this book focuses on. It can create tension, conflicts, and sacrifice, and it can also create mutual growth, fulfillment, and harmony. My research describes the paths that lead to these different outcomes.

My focus on dual-career couples means that most of the people I interviewed are middle-class. While this sample does not reflect the whole of society, it is an important group because, for better or worse, members of the middle class tend to set the norms for other classes in the realm of relationships and work.[11] This group has the luxury of options and opportunities to improve their lives that few other classes enjoy. Yet this luxury is often accompanied by anxiety and turbulence.[12] It is this combination of opportunity and turbulence that allowed me as a researcher to see the challenges these couples face and the deeper psychological and social forces that underpin them.

Almost everyone I interviewed asked to remain anonymous. To respect their wishes, I changed every person's name, where the couples live, and other features that may identify them, such as gender and names of their children. People's occupations are so intimately tied to their stories that these are mainly unchanged; the organizations in which they work, however, have been disguised. But all of the events—the decisions each couple made; the actions they took; the frustrating, exhilarating, and occasionally wild things that happened to them—are as they were told to me.

Although this book is based on rigorous qualitative research and analysis, I do not pretend that the way I have systematized couples' experiences and dilemmas is objectively or factually true.

Like all social scientists, my work attempts to capture people's subjective experiences in a way that makes them understandable and relatable without losing their humanity. My aim throughout the book is to highlight the commonalities among couples and lay out an approach that has something to offer all.

Charting Your Own Path

My research reveals that while couples who successfully navigate their transitions make radically different choices, they share a common approach. As a result, this book focuses on *how* couples can best work through their transitions, and not on *what* specific choices they should make or life structure they should adopt. This focus on process and approach will allow you to make mindful life decisions and understand their consequences, all while maintaining a solid relationship.

Following my approach to tackle the three transitions won't make the challenges of life for a dual-career couple disappear. But it can increase your chances of enjoying long-term growth and fulfilment in your careers, your family life, and your relationship.

If you and a partner are seeking ways to enjoy richer, more rewarding careers while also nurturing a deep and lasting relationship, this book is for you. There is no such thing as the perfect dual-career couple—life is too complex and unpredictable for that. But understanding the challenges ahead, the transitions you will face, and the tools for communication, problem solving, negotiation, and mutual support that other couples have found useful can increase your chances not just of surviving, but also of thriving.

How Can
We Make
This Work?

2

When the Honeymoon Ends

Let's return to Cheryl and Mark.

Five years before baby Annabel was born—as you may remember from chapter 1, just twenty-four hours before Mark quit his corporate job to join a friend's startup—Mark and Cheryl had met in Chicago. Mutual friends set them up on a blind date, ice-skating on a freezing December day. She was working in a bank, he in a software company.

In those years, they rarely discussed their careers and made ample time for their friends—both had attended college in the city and had a broad social network. Like many new couples fortunate enough to have two good jobs in their early thirties, they worked hard and played hard. Marriage did not change that. After their wedding, they purchased a small apartment and kept their busy rhythm going. They felt they had it all.

By the time Annabel came along, Mark had spent ten years in the software company and longed for change. He had a passion for geolocalization technology, was a skilled programmer, and had always had the itch to work at a startup. But he had never found the right opportunity. He watched with envy as friends took the leap and wondered, with increasing frustration, when his time might come.

While Cheryl understood his unfulfilled desire, she was more focused on a different project, one that they shared as a couple—having children. After six months of trying, they got pregnant and were over the moon. The nine months before the birth flew by. It was all they could do to upgrade their apartment before Annabel arrived. When Mark was invited to join a startup the day after the birth, it was unexpected.

But while for Mark it was a no-brainer, Cheryl felt caught. Neither could anticipate the full consequences.

When I spoke with them seven years later, Cheryl and Mark agreed that this moment marked the start of a major transition in their lives—the real start of their life as a couple. In a matter of days, they went from being two independent spirits, enjoying their work and excited about their expanding lives, into stressed-out new parents struggling to make sense of their careers and of their relationship.

Five weeks after giving birth, Cheryl was back at work. But now her main emotion was no longer the enjoyment of tackling tough challenges and working with clients, but rather resentment over being separated from her baby to support her husband's dreams. Meanwhile, Mark was pouring every hour into making the startup a success while being racked with guilt about neglecting his wife and daughter. Petty bickering descended into serious conflicts. By the time Annabel was nine months old, Cheryl and Mark were in counseling, trying to save their marriage.

Cheryl and Mark's story is unique in its details, but it follows a predictable pattern. Life, love, and work seem to be going great for both partners, then something happens in one domain that has consequences for others, and life quickly spirals out of control.

While many of the couples in my research recognized this pattern and had seen others fall into it, few of them anticipated it when they first fell in love.

The Honeymoon Period

Falling in love and starting a new relationship is wonderful. Whether you are living it now or thinking back to the early years of your relationship, you know the heady feeling of those days: the long romantic walks, the endless phone calls, the realization that the other person is *the one*. Couples invest heavily in their relationship during these early days, showering each other with attention, time, and kindness. Like Cheryl and Mark's early days, the honeymoon period for many couples is plain sailing.

While couples can form at any life stage—and the emotional experience of falling in love is the same whether a person is eighteen or eighty-eight—becoming a couple peaks in the mid-twenties to mid-thirties.[1] In this and chapters 3 and 4, I'm going to focus on this life stage because it is the one that most often coincides with a dual-career couple's first transition. That said, the dynamics of this transition are the same whatever age you face it—and all new couples face it eventually, whether it's their first serious relationship or a new relationship being built after a previous one ends.

The couples in my sample who got together in their twenties and thirties described a period in which they heavily invested in their relationship and their careers. While many used their early twenties to test out different career options, by the time they hit the tail end of that decade, they were generally more set on a direction, focused on proving their potential, and laying the foundation of a career track. Keen to succeed, they put in long hours, accepted extra assignments, and relished their progress.

People who can dedicate themselves fully to their careers in their twenties are what I call *unbounded talent*. They have few personal responsibilities or constraints like a mortgage, children, or elderly relatives that compete for their time or bind them to a specific location. Leveraging these young people's desire to establish their careers and their unboundedness, most organizations and bosses ply people at this life and career stage with opportunities to prove themselves. And because of their unboundedness at this stage, I found that they are likely to accept almost everything without pushing back.

When unbounded talents first become a couple, their careers often proceed on parallel tracks, at least for a while, with relatively little friction. Their understanding of, and fresh love for, each other makes it easy for partners to offer each other kindness and support. If one needs to work late every night for a month, the other can use the free time to catch up with friends, family, or work or focus on hobbies. Even if one partner needs to take a short-term project in a different city or country, the couple is likely enough to view it as an opportunity to travel rather than a strain on family life.

Blossoming love and work lives make the honeymoon period a time of possibility and excitement. A relative lack of constraints, an abundance of tolerance, and a willingness to discount challenges free couples up to do what they need and want, and they often do a lot. On top of a busy career and fulfilling love life, I found that couples kept up the pursuits of their early twenties, be they sports, socializing, volunteering, or hobbies. Youthful energy made socializing or traveling on weekends energizing, not depleting. The world felt full of possibilities to these couples, and they felt that they could grab them all.

When I ask dual-career couples in their forties whether they can have it all, most roll their eyes. But when I ask dual-career couples in their late twenties, they are likely to say that they have heard the arguments, read the articles, and may even logically accept that most couples cannot have it all. But, they add, "We're different, right? We are lucky, we have each other, and we work hard. Perhaps most couples can't have it all, but we can." That is the powerful illusion that a promising career start and a blossoming love foster.

Having It All

When I first met Malcolm and Helen, they had been together for eighteen months. Malcolm worked in operations at a local airport, and Helen as an engineer in a chemical processing plant. Malcolm's hours were regular but antisocial, as he often began his shift early in the morning. Helen sometimes worked nights and weekend shifts. But with no other commitments, they spent all their time together when neither was working, and their relationship flourished. Both had large families who lived locally, and they enjoyed spending time with them and friends. They also kept up the hobbies they had cultivated in their early twenties. Malcolm was an active member of his local hockey club, and Helen a dedicated volunteer at a weekend retreat center for disabled children.

Although both were anxious about their career prospects—Malcolm feeling that he should be progressing faster, and Helen worrying about the volatility of the chemicals industry—they were very content with life. As she told me, "I have everything I've ever wanted in life." Malcolm talked about their future, too. It included a wedding planned for the next year, a family to follow, and plenty of career ambitions for both of them. He reflected, "We both have a lot of energy and are well organized. I know some people struggle. But given how our lives are now, I really cannot see any major issues ahead." Helen and Malcolm felt they had it all and, when I first spoke to them, assumed that this feeling would continue with little conflict and struggle over the long term.

It's easy to dismiss Malcolm and Helen as naive. Yet many young professionals hold similar assumptions about their future during the honeymoon period of relationships. As human beings, we are hardwired to build assumptions about the world based on our personal experiences.[2] Many dual-career couples in their honeymoon period build the assumption that they can have it all because it reflects the world they currently live in. They are aware of the good fortune of having two independent careers and assume that as long as they work hard and stick together, they really can have it all. For the first few years of their relationship, many of the couples I spoke to felt like they did. Why would that not continue?

Triggers of the First Transition

An unexpected layoff, a geographic relocation, an international assignment, a major career opportunity, a new baby, a serious illness, a decision to join two families from previous marriages—these are all major life events that can upend couples' lives, marking the end of their honeymoon period and the start of their first transition. Needless to say, couples face many major life events throughout their lives together. The first, however, holds special importance because to accommodate to it, couples can no longer maintain independent career and life paths—they must join those paths into one.

Of all the triggers that trigger couples' first transition, two types are prevalent for those in their twenties and thirties. Both are joyful in nature and yet require major accommodations in couples' personal and working lives. The first is a career opportunity for one partner that presents hard choices for the couple. The second is the arrival of a new child. Let us start with the first one, as faced by Jasmine and Alejandro, a typical early-stage couple whom I spoke to five years after their first transition began. I'm going to introduce their story here and then continue it in chapter 3, where we'll find out what they decided to do and the consequences of their choice.

The couple met in their late twenties in Toronto, where Alejandro worked in production planning at a car manufacturer and Jasmine was an engineer in a renewable energy firm. For the first three years, their relationship flourished and their careers prospered in parallel. Then, just as they were planning their wedding, Jasmine was unexpectedly offered her dream promotion—to join a team charged with designing a new hydroelectric power plant. The promotion would put Jasmine at the cutting edge of her field, provide plenty of learning, and likely accelerate her career. The downside? It was based in Vancouver.

Jasmine and Alejandro knew that living more than twenty-seven hundred miles apart was not for them. But what should they do? Alejandro's company had no office in Vancouver. He considered resigning and looking for a job on the West Coast. She considered forgoing the promotion. Neither seemed a good option for their respective careers, and they could not see an obvious third way. Accustomed to having it all, Alejandro and Jasmine did not want to hurt their careers, but separating was out of the question. Until this point, they had never discussed the possibility of leaving Toronto or thought of their careers as anything but independent. Suddenly they found themselves paralyzed by the choice and unable to decide how to move forward.

Because careers are increasingly mobile, more and more couples are facing a choice like Jasmine and Alejandro's. Forty years ago, the choice would have been straightforward for most couples—the man's career would have taken priority. Nowadays, couples are more egalitarian, and few apply such a rudimental decision criterion. Careers have also become more uncertain, making it harder for couples to predict the long-term consequences of their choices: *What if we move across country to follow our partner's job only for them to get laid off a year later?* All this change can turn great career opportunities into nerve-racking challenges for dual-career couples.

The second most common trigger of the first transition that early-stage couples encounter is the birth of a child. A happy event for sure, it is nevertheless one that upends couples' assumptions about parallel career paths and having it all. Let's meet another couple, Haru and Sana, whose story I'll also introduce here and revisit in chapter 3.

Haru and Sana excitedly awaited the birth of their first child, Airi. When she arrived on a cold February morning in Tokyo, her parents had read a pile of baby books and were confident that they knew what to expect. Although it's relatively untraditional in Japan for mothers to continue their careers, Haru and Sana belonged to a new generation challenging old norms. They reserved a place in a day-care facility located close to their office, and Haru's mother, who lived close by, was available to lend an extra hand when required. Yet as new parents often discover, Haru and Sana quickly realized that even if they had read all the baby books ever published, they could never have anticipated how the birth of Airi would impact their lives and change their outlook.

Haru had two days of paternity leave, and Sana five months of maternity leave before returning to the e-commerce giant where they both worked. Neither wanted to skip a beat in their careers, but they still needed to drop off and pick up Airi from day care, not to mention make it through the sleepless nights. They felt guilty when they left Airi each morning; both wanted to spend more time with their growing girl. They also felt the weight of societal expectations that babies are "best with their mothers."

Should Sana have taken a career break, they wondered, or gone part-time? Both sets of grandparents dropped subtle hints that perhaps it would be best.

While she was a fiercely dedicated mother, Sana had witnessed many friends dropping out of their careers "for a while" never to return to work, and she didn't want to sacrifice hers. She began to resent Haru. Their careers were at a similar stage, but she did much more of the housework and parenting than he did, and he was never subjected to the kinds of guilt trips she regularly experienced. Their exhaustion exacerbated tensions, and the carefree days of their honeymoon period receded into a very distant past. From feeling that they had it all, they moved to wondering how they could make it work.

———————

With rare exceptions, the triggers of the first transition for couples in their twenties and thirties signal progression in their careers and lives. Whether it's relatively straightforward events such as a relocation or a new child faced by early-stage couples, or more complex ones faced by couples who get together later in life, such as how to join two families from previous marriages, the transition they trigger is similar.

How Can We Make This Work?

Whatever trigger brings the honeymoon period to an end, it reveals the nature of a couple's first transition: accommodating not just to the new life that the event opens up, but to each other in a new way. That is, to move from having parallel, independent careers and lives to having interdependent ones. When couples have interdependent careers and lives, they mutually rely on each other to be successful and fulfilled. The move to interdependence raises the defining question of the first transition: *How can we make this work?* Or put another way, *How can we structure our lives to allow both of us to thrive in love and in work?* Answering this question is the developmental task of couples in their first transition.

Couples that work figure out the answer to this defining question deliberately, together. Doing so requires them to negotiate how to prioritize their careers and divide family commitments. As a result, couples craft a joint path to travel on that replaces their two previously independent ones.

In chapter 3, I will explain the traps that ensnare couples as they try to accommodate the major life event they face. I will also illustrate the struggle most couples face while moving through their transition. Then, in chapter 4, I will address how couples can successfully craft a joint path that deliberately accommodates their unique situation and carries them out of their first transition and to the next phase of their lives. Along the way we'll see how Mark and Cheryl's, Jasmine and Alejandro's, and Sana and Haru's stories unfold. Before we do so, however, I want to share a tool that can set you up well for this and the next transitions.

Couple Contracting

Couples that work, I found, make choices deliberately—that is, openly and jointly—rather than implicitly and one for the other. This way of choosing, as we will see, is fundamental for the transitions not to leave issues left over that will come back to bite you. It is thus crucial that couples have the instruments to deliberate together what to do; for example, to accommodate to a major life event, as in the case of the first transition.

Let me start by sharing my first encounter with what I would much later realize is a "tool" that many couples use in these circumstances, whether they even regard it as a tool or not. Four weeks after Gianpiero and I got together, I boarded a plane for his hometown in Sicily. It was December 27—we had decided it was a little early for an extended family Christmas. I landed into a sunny day and was whisked off to a nearby fishing village on the back of his old red Vespa. I'm not making this up. As we sat on a small cliff watching the waves, Gianpiero pulled out a notepad and two pens and said, "I really want to make this work." We had both had our fair share of failed relationships in the distant and very recent past. "So why don't we do this mindfully?" he added.

We spent the next few hours first writing, then discussing, what we thought we wanted from our relationship, from each other, and from our life together. We also talked about our concerns for the future. It was powerful, insightful, and—people laugh when I say this—unexpectedly romantic. It was a conversation that grounded our beginning and one that we return to periodically. We still have the paper we wrote on.

Throughout my research, I have kept coming back to our conversations and have used insights from other couples to develop a more systematic tool: *couple contracting*. It is not designed to tackle specific challenges (I'll share ideas on that as the chapters unfold). Instead, it is designed to help you be deliberate in your transitions. I'm describing it here because the earlier couples get into the habit of using it, the smoother their transitions seem to be. It is, however, a tool that can help couples at all life stages.

Couple contracting involves in-depth discussions of three areas—values, boundaries, and fears. Negotiating and finding common ground in all three gives couples borders and direction for the path that they will walk together. It also helps couples navigate difficult decisions because it surfaces agreed-upon criteria in advance. It is important that you develop a good understanding of your partner's positions and find some common ground, but there is no need to agree on every single point.

VALUES. What makes you happy and proud? What gives you satisfaction? What makes for a good life? These are all questions that can help you figure out what you believe matters most. People use values to assess whether their life is turning out the way they want. When our choices and actions align with our values, we feel content. When they don't, we feel stressed and unhappy. If openly discussed, values can help determine your priorities. For example, if you and your partner both value family time highly, neither of you should take a job that requires seventy-hour workweeks.

When asked if they share values, most couples quickly answer yes. This tends to be true for high-level values—family, integrity, friends, and so on—but there can be surprising differences in how people define those terms. Take one couple I spoke to. Both claimed the same values—work hard, play hard, and have a good family life. But when I dug deeper and asked them to describe what those words meant, a good family life for him meant stability, whereas for her, who had traveled a lot with her family as a child, it meant adventure. Unsurprisingly, their family life was tense, but unable to spot the root cause of the tension, they found it hard to break through their deadlock.

BOUNDARIES. Setting clear boundaries reduces uncertainty and eases decision making. It's helpful to consider three types of boundaries—place, time, and presence. Many people whose careers are mobile have places they would love to work and live in at least for a period. You may want to be based in a certain location to raise your children, another as you get closer to retirement. There may be places you would prefer to avoid. Careers also demand a lot of our time. People face periods where they have to put in more hours than they would like, such as a time-critical project or the run-up to a big promotion. But how much is too much work? Finally, and related to time, is physical presence. Would you and your partner be fine with taking jobs in different cities and living apart for a period? What about short-term secondments and job swaps? How much work travel is too much, and how will you juggle travel between you? What is the minimum amount of time you want to spend together?

Negotiating boundaries narrows choices, which can feel restrictive. Yet scores of studies have proven that having fewer (not more) options makes it easier to choose and makes us happier with our choices.[3] Decades of research confirm that clear boundaries make people feel psychologically safe and more likely to experiment and grow.[4] Boundaries also reduce room for disappointment and regret in relationships.

Many MBA students I meet are fortunate enough to face a raft of career options. For those in couples, the wealth of options can create real headaches if they have no agreed-upon boundaries. A few years ago, one of my students came to see me, dejected. He had gotten what, in his words was, "the job of my dreams"—running the African office of a major NGO in Kenya. His excitement, though, quickly turned to disappointment when his wife told him that she could never move their family to Kenya. Why, I asked, did he pursue that option if it was a no-go for his wife? He explained that, faced with so much uncertainty, they had thought it best that he apply to everything, see what offers he got, and then make the decision together. Their lack of advanced boundary setting had inadvertently set them up for conflict and disappointment.

FEARS. Much like the canaries that miners once used to warn of gas leaks, explicitly discussing fears can help you spot when your relationship is entering dangerous territory. It can also lead you to take preemptive actions to ensure that your fears are not realized. There are a host of fears you might have about your relationship and careers. You may worry that your partner's family will encroach on your relationship, that over time the two of you will grow apart, that your partner will have an affair, that you will have to sacrifice your career for your partner's, that you may not be able to have children. The list can seem endless. Yet, as the Roman philosopher Seneca wrote, "We suffer more from imagination than from reality."

When couples give themselves permission to think and talk about their fears, three things happen. First, they build greater mutual sensitivity and support. If you know that your partner is worried about the role of your parents in your lives, you are more likely to sensitively manage the boundary between them and your couple. Second, you can figure out some warning signs to look out for to recognize if your fears are in danger of becoming less imaginary. For example, if you are worried about growing apart over time, you might agree to sound the alarm if you don't have at least two date nights a month. Finally, you can take some steps to mitigate these fears. If you are interested in a risky career transition but worried that financial commitments could prevent it, you might agree to cut back on family spending in order to build a financial buffer.

Taken together, negotiating and finding common ground in the three areas of values, boundaries, and fears will help you shape your joint path. The values define its direction, the boundaries set its borders, and the fears make you aware of potential cliffs on either side and invite you to keep your steps on the path. Having clarity on these three domains will make it easier for you to negotiate and overcome the challenges you will inevitably encounter, whichever one of the three transitions you are in.

The thought of couple contracting makes some feel nervous: *What if my partner and I disagree? What if it sparks conflict and relationship strife?* The fact is, hard shared choices in life are never made through easy conversations. My research shows that while these conversations can feel a little stilted, couples who shape their relationship deliberately through them find them an integral and meaningful part of their lives.

I recently received an email from a woman who, having seen me present the idea, embraced couple contracting in a novel way. She explained that six months previously, she had fallen in love with a man whom she had met on a holiday in South Africa. Two intercontinental trips and thousands of Skype hours later, their relationship was blossoming. But the thought of the future was daunting, and they studiously avoided discussing it—until, that is, she suggested they try couple contracting. They arranged a Skype date that turned into what she described as "the most meaningful three hours of my life." For the first time, they talked about how their paths would join and how they could build a journey through life together. They agreed that he would look for career opportunities in London, but in the long term, they wanted to spend a period of their lives together in South Africa. They talked about the importance of children, their fears about a cross-cultural marriage, and their commitment to living together permanently.

These two people were more than eight thousand miles apart and only six months into their relationship when they began couple contracting. One might say that they became a couple through it. Perhaps all couples truly begin when both people share values, boundaries, and fears and find that their lives are better if they continue sharing them. The best time for any couple to have these conversations is now. The sooner the better. It might be over Skype, curled up together on the sofa, on a long walk in the countryside, or in a Sicilian fishing village. It doesn't matter where these conversations happen. Making them an integral part of your relationship will reap rewards. It's unrealistic to expect your values, boundaries, and fears to remain static over the course of your relationship. So revisiting it every year or at every major transition is wise.

How to Talk

Couple contracting is a guide to *what* to talk about, but *how* to talk about it is a different question. When things are going well and the topic is uncontroversial, most couples find it easy to talk. But when times are tense and the topic heated, communication can be a minefield. Luckily, there is much research on what makes communication between partners effective and what can hijack it. First, let's look at the damaging patterns that you should avoid.

There are many ways to sabotage communication and hence your relationship. Psychologist John Gottman identified four particularly damaging behaviors that he called the *four horsemen of the apocalypse,* for their ability to ruin marriages:[5]

> *Contempt* is the most destructive pattern because it conveys that you don't respect your partner and that you think yourself superior. Behaviors that signal contempt include mimicking, sarcasm, mocking, eye-rolling, and sneering. Contempt occurs when we dismiss and denigrate the other's feelings. It is the opposite of empathy.

> *Criticism* usually starts out small. People pick out and condemn minor details of their partner's behavior or appearance. But it soon escalates, making your partner feel resentful and controlled. Criticism devalues the other and signals that they should submit to your will. In the face of criticism, our partners usually resist, and the cycle of control and resistance kills cooperation.

> *Defensiveness.* People act defensively without knowing it, and everyone does when their partner is contemptuous or critical. Without realizing it, most of us believe that when our partner does something that hurts, it is intentional, but when we do the same thing, it is inadvertent. This double

standard means that when we act defensively, our partner responds defensively, creating a vicious circle that destroys intimacy.

Stonewalling is the total refusal to discuss or consider your partner's perspective. Retorts that signal stonewalling include "Just leave me alone . . . " "End of discussion . . . " and "Just do whatever you want . . ." Sometimes people stonewall in response to contempt and criticism; other times they do it to avoid difficult conversations. Either way, stonewalling isolates you from your partner.

You may recognize some of these patterns. Perhaps you become overly critical when your temper frays. Maybe your partner stonewalls you when the conversation turns to certain topics. There are almost certainly times when both of you are defensive. How can you counteract these destructive patters of interaction? The answer is rather simple, yet hard to follow. Kindness. Of all the things that can help communication, kindness stands out as the most important predictor of satisfaction in a partnership.[6]

Kindness and Attention

You can express kindness in two ways. The first is through small acts of generosity and consideration. Letting your partner sleep in while you get the kids up, making them a morning coffee, rubbing their shoulders after a hard day at work, taking an interest in their favorite hobby, buying small unexpected gifts. In the early days of relationships, many of us do such things freely, but as time goes by and we become busy, we start taking our partner for granted and our generosity at times erodes, or at least appears to.

The second way you express kindness is being generous about your partner's intentions. What do you think when your partner forgets to pick up milk and bread on their way home from work? It's easy to flick into blame mode, attribute it to their laziness or carelessness, and criticize them. It is harder to recognize that they just absentmindedly forgot because they were mulling over a stressful issue at work.

In couples where kindness abounds, both partners see each other as decent people who have the other's best interests at heart. Believing your partner has good intentions means that when they do let you down, you are more likely to attribute it to an external event—work stress, traffic, and the like—and not blame them. Likewise, when your partner does something kind, you are likely to attribute it to them being a good person.[7] Both assumptions lead to a more satisfying relationship.

Perhaps the best thing about kindness is that it is contagious. If you are kind to your partner, they are likely to mirror you and be kind in response.[8] Just as defensiveness creates a vicious cycle, kindness creates a virtuous cycle in a relationship. Kindness is powerful because it sets the stage for effective communication. If you assume your partner has good intentions, then you are unlikely to be defensive. Likewise, if you are kind to each other, there will be no space for contempt or criticism.

All couples sometimes communicate in negative ways. None of us is perfect. What psychologists find important is not whether we communicate in negative ways, but the ratio of negative to positive communication. A classic study found that a 5:1 ratio (or more) of positives to negatives sets couples on a good track.[9] This is not an exact science, so there is no need to stick a scorecard to the kitchen fridge. It is, however, a good rule of thumb to see whether your communication ratio needs a kindness boost.

My work with couples has revealed another important factor that is in short supply these days—undivided attention. In our busy, hyperconnected world, it is increasingly rare that couples give each other 100 percent of their attention. People almost always have an electronic device competing for their attention, not to mention TV, phone calls, and that long to-do list that buzzes in the back of their minds. Yet undivided attention is the fuel of relationships. And it's a very powerful fuel.

When presenting my work to groups, I sometimes run an exercise in which each partner asks the other a simple question; for example "How was your day?" Then for three minutes, they simply listen to the response. No interrupting, no questions, no comments, no talking. Full, undivided active listening—body and soul. The impact is heartening. Looking around the room, I can see people's bodies opening up to each other, deep eye contact, and looks of empathy, joy, and connection, all in three minutes. Afterward, people describe feeling understood, valued, and intimate—the feelings we crave in our relationships. They also disclose more to their partners. This exercise shows that it doesn't take hours. Small pockets of undivided attention make a huge difference in a relationship. After all, who cannot afford three minutes of love?

We are all at times guilty of riding one of the four horsemen of the apocalypse. We can also be kind and think kindly of our partner and give them undivided attention. The more you lean in the direction of the latter, the easier your conversations will become. Practicing this way of being together will not just help you with couple contracting and your daily interactions, it will increase the holistic quality of your relationship.

3

Struggling to
Do It All

Twins bathed, fed, and asleep—check. Urgent work emails dealt with—check. Bag packed for tomorrow's work trip—check. Hannah collapsed onto the sofa after another long day, finally able to catch her breath. Santiago joined her a few moments later, and Hannah took his hand, happy they'd finally have a few moments together. But when he avoided her eyes, she realized that something was wrong.

"What is it?" she asked.

"Oh, nothing," Santiago replied. But he continued to look away, and suddenly Hannah realized that his eyes were welling with tears.

"What is it?" she asked again, this time with alarm.

"I'm sorry," Santiago said, his voice breaking. "It's just that I've realized—we're never going to live in Portugal, are we?" Now his chest was heaving, racked by sobs. Neither he nor Hannah were prepared for his depth of emotion.

Six years earlier, Hannah and Santiago had met at a conference, enjoyed a dinner together that turned into a weekend of romance, and fallen in love. For eighteen months, they had managed a long-distance relationship from their hometowns of Lisbon and Brussels, traveling together during holiday weeks and spending hours on the phone while apart. They knew they belonged together. But how and where?

After endless discussion, the issue was brought to a head when Hannah became pregnant with twins. Santiago and Hannah suddenly needed to make a location decision, and fast, if they were going to make their new family work. "We were rabbits in the headlights," Hannah recounted, "The most important thing was to make a decision." Up against the wall, they resorted to economic criteria to decide where to make their home.

"Hannah was earning more, so joining her in Belgium was a no-brainer. Or so it seemed at the time," Santiago recalled. They got married, and he found a job at a small firm in Brussels. But as Hannah's career took off, Santiago's stagnated. Being a foreigner was tough at his firm, and he was repeatedly passed over for promotion. By the time the twins turned two, the salary gap between Hannah and Santiago had widened.

Career woes weren't the only thing troubling Santiago. Their lives had become what he described as "a frantic cycle of do, do, do." They both worked hard and were hands-on parents. Gone were the long meandering Sunday morning walks they had used to take through Brussels's city parks. Gone the spontaneous nights out. But most saddening of all, gone was the deep intimacy he and Hannah shared in their early days.

Their intimacy was replaced by a creeping sense of loneliness that made him realize how important the culture and customs of his homeland were for him. The people in Belgium were perfectly nice, yet somehow there was an emotional gulf between him and them that made real friendship seem impossible. Santiago found himself dreaming about the foods, the sights, even the characteristic smells of Lisbon. He was deeply homesick—and his love for Hannah wasn't enough to sustain him.

Santiago longed to return to Portugal, get his career back on track, and move to a slower pace of life. Yet based on the economic criteria they'd agreed upon, that option was off the table. Santiago was full of regret, and Hannah of guilt. "I felt I'd cornered him," she confessed. Santiago's emotional outpouring on the sofa was the first time the two realized that the way they had made their couple work had trapped them on a path with which neither were happy. Their rational analysis and economic decision criteria, combined with their subsequent incessant "doing," was ensuring that neither could thrive.

The Panic Zone

The major life event that triggers the first transition throws couples like Hannah and Santiago into the panic zone. Stress and uncertainty replace the harmony and excitement of the honeymoon period. The delight in having it all is replaced by the fear of not being able to make it work. As tensions rise, petty arguments increase. This is a time when many couples have their first serious conflicts.

I found that couples' urgency to move away from the panic zone as quickly as possible can lead them into traps that prolong the struggle of the first transition. The traps—relying on economic decision criteria, focusing on the short term, concentrating on the practical, and striving to do it all—are like decoys. They appear to lead to an interdependent joint path. They appear to answer the question, *How can we make this work?* But in reality, and as Santiago and Hannah's story illustrates, they make couples accommodate to their major life event in ways that stores up regrets for later.

How long couples spend in their period of struggle, how severe the struggle becomes, and indeed whether they make it out depends on their ability to recognize and overcome these traps.

Trap 1: Economic Decision Criteria

Overrelying on economic decision criteria was a common trap for couples in my sample who were negotiating their first transition. They chose the location they lived in, the career that was prioritized, and the person who did proportionally more child care to maximize economic gain. This choice seemed deliberate but wasn't truly so because it subordinated couples' values and desires to economic imperatives that were often, when looked at closely, excuses for conforming to traditional social demands.

Using money as one decision criteria is sensible, of course, especially when you are short of options and resources. But few people live for financial gain alone. In their careers, people are also motivated by continual learning, deepening their expertise, and growing their responsibilities. Couples are attracted to a location because of proximity to family, the quality of life it affords, and their ability to build a strong community. People also have preferences for time spent with their children and pursuing their personal interests.

Hannah and Santiago's story shows that ignoring the importance of these other motivators sets couples up for problems in the future. Their story also illustrates how hard the economic decision criteria trap is to escape. Deciding to live in Belgium because Hannah earned more money stifled Santiago's opportunities to gain promotions and salary raises because he was a foreigner in a firm operating mostly in a local market. This choice in turn slowed his career and widened the earnings gap between the two of them. The widened gap made it even more important that they stay in Belgium to maintain their income level and made a move appear less sensible and, at times, not feasible at all.

The dynamic of economic decision criteria cementing a suboptimal arrangement doesn't only concern location decisions. Overly focusing on money is one reason why couples move from two careers to one. The mid- to late thirties is a peak time for such movement and typically coincides with the birth of a second or third child. On average, 31 percent of mothers opt out of their careers to care for children, and they do so for a median of two years.[1] Some women genuinely want to opt out to focus full-time on their families, and they never regret it. There is, however, a larger proportion of women who feel they should opt out for a period, and who subsequently regret that choice and its implications.[2]

So why do women opt out when they don't want to? There is a complex web of reasons. Societal expectations of intensive mothering, unsupportive husbands, unsupportive bosses, and an overload of tasks at home are all contributing factors.[3] But the tipping point can come when women calculate the cost of child care against what they earn. "So much of my salary went to child care, I just got to the point where I felt, 'Why bother?'" This is a phrase often heard by those who study women who opt out, and one that I frequently encountered in my research for this book. That's not to say that finances are the only or most important reason, but they are often used as a rationale.

––––––––––

With two children under three, Pete and Susan were frazzled. Susan liked her job in her company's audit department, but at the end of one stressful month, she calculated that the cost of her girls' day care was a significant chunk of her post-tax earnings and wondered why she kept working. Why stay in a tough job and struggle through the overwhelming logistical demands of having small children while working full-time if most her salary went to child care? That night, she showed her calculation to Pete and declared her intention to take a four-year career break until the girls started elementary school. Pete knew how important Susan's career was to her and worried that she would be unfulfilled, but he wanted to support her. He also knew that if she took a career break, it would ease the family logistics strain and make little difference to their finances. Together they decided that it was the right option for them.

Fast-forward four years. Susan was struggling to reenter her career at the same level. She eventually accepted a lower-level position at a smaller company, with a 20 percent pay cut. She lamented, "If I had known the career and financial hit I would take beforehand, I would definitely have made different decisions. It's ironic that as a trained auditor, my calculations were so off."

Pete and Susan's story is backed up by a wealth of research showing that it seldom pays for a spouse to quit their job. Women who take more than three years off face up to a 37 percent pay cut when they return.[4] The baby and toddler years seem long when you're in them, but they are only a small proportion of a forty-plus-year career. Studies have estimated that the compounded financial loss of opting out over the rest of a lifetime can be more than a $1 million.[5]

The moral of this story is not that you should never opt out. It is that you should never do so for financial reasons, or more precisely social pressure, alone. Whatever challenge you are facing, economic criteria alone don't lead to good decisions. Instead, they lead you into unexpected challenges. If you are facing your first transition, it is vital that you take time to deliberate the decision criteria that are important to you. These might include some of the following life, relationship, and career factors: living close (or far) from family, having a network of friends and a strong community, promotion prospects, a chance to grow skills and expertise, and having a healthy work-life balance.

Deliberating criteria before you make any decision is critical. In the stress and urgency of the panic zone, it's tempting to view these discussions as a luxury, but they hold the power to mitigate future regrets and help you more mindfully craft a joint path. The second moral of this story is that what seems to make economic sense in the short term often does not in the long term. Which brings us to the second trap of the first transition—short-term bias.

Trap 2: Short-Term Bias

When couples rushed to make decisions to combine their lives and careers, I found that they tended to overlook long-term implications. They were so caught up in escaping the panic zone and moving back to a more comfortable space that their thinking became anchored on immediate issues. This short-term focus is a common decision-making bias.[6] It may lead to a joint path that works temporarily; however, that path is likely to be littered with challenges that couples didn't anticipate and that will hinder them in the future.

Let's return to the example of opting out. Maybe you are committed to opting out for a period and it works for you and your partner, irrespective of the financial implications. At the point of opting out, people naturally focus on the short-term family benefits—precious time spent with children and more bandwidth to take care of everything else at home. If they consider the long-term implications at all, they assume they will reenter their career where they left off, perhaps with a little retraining but otherwise without major issue. The research reveals a very different picture.

Once people opt out of their career, they are often blocked out from returning. Recruiters perceive job applicants who have opted out as less dedicated, less reliable, and thus less worthy of hiring. This perception is even worse for men who opt out when compared with women.[7] One study found that stay-at-home parents were less likely to be hired than applicants who had been laid off from their previous job.[8] The uphill battle this prejudice creates for people wanting to opt back in means that they often don't return to their former careers, but instead move into different ones.[9] Another study of working mothers showed that 93 percent of those surveyed wanted to return to their careers, but only 40 percent succeeded in returning to full-time work.[10]

The short-term focus that plagues couples in the panic zone means that they fail to make plans for how they might opt back in when the time is right. It doesn't have to be that way. One physiotherapist I spoke to impressed me with her farsightedness. After giving birth to her second child, she wanted to be a full-time mom for a period but was worried about the career implications. Not wanting to be sidelined, she registered as a replacement physiotherapist to cover sickness and holidays for her former colleagues while she took a three-year career break. She worked an average of three days a month, just enough to keep her in touch with colleagues and up-to-date while still dedicating most of her time to her young family. At the end of her break, she was able to move back into her old job. At first, she had a little less responsibility, but she was quickly back on track.

There is plenty of research about the long-term implications of opting out and back in, but those implications often seem unclear and hard to predict when you are making other decisions. If you change jobs to follow your partner, will you thrive in your new position or will you regret the transition and resent your partner? If you both go for international assignments, will it really boost your careers or simply make it hard to come home?

On the one hand, it's impossible to scope out and predict every implication when making hard choices. Sketching the pros and cons will not magically point to the best way forward. None of us can predict the future. On the other hand, some long-term implications matter more than others. And those that matter most are the implications that our choices have on who we will become—the identity implications.

Hard choices present us with windows into parallel universes where we become different versions of ourselves in our couple. Will we become the work-hard, play-hard, adventure couple who travel the world, or will we become the stable career couple who are nested in a community of family and friends? Will we become the do-it-all couple who continually juggle family and careers, or will we become the divide-and-conquer family in which one partner takes the lead career and the other the lead family role? Will we become the fast-paced city couple who drink lattes and join the yoga studio, or the outdoorsy countryside couple into mountain biking and wilderness camping?

Without forethought, identity implications only become apparent a few years after you have made your choices. Many people I interviewed for this book described waking up one morning with the sudden realization that they were living a life they had never anticipated and had become a person they didn't want to be—that their decisions had made them, instead of them making their decisions.

Considering who a decision will make you become is especially helpful for couples in cross-cultural relationships. Once a rarity, more of us are now choosing partners from a different culture. Even if not from another country, your partner may be from another region that has a different culture, outlook on life, and even language. One of the thorniest identity issues such couples face is the question of home.

As Hannah and Santiago's story illustrates, home is an emotional question. Some of us never quite feel ourselves when we are not in the place we were brought up as children. Others actively try to avoid that place and build a home elsewhere. Still more are satisfied being away from home for long periods, but when children arrive or retirement looms, the call of home rings loudly. Depending on your and your partner's feelings about home, different choices will make sense. Some couples choose to live in one person's home region, others split their time between the two, and others choose a third, more neutral territory to build a new home. Whatever the outcome, and especially if you are in a cross-cultural relationship, it's vital that you tackle the question of home early on. If not, don't be surprised if you land in Hannah and Santiago's dilemma.

What taking an identity perspective shows us is that the most practical, rational, or financially optimal choice may not be the one that leads you to a joint path on which you can both thrive. Without considering the identity implications of your choices, you drift into a path that doesn't quite feel yours. Considering identity implications is the way you become the author of your life story. Unexpected things will always happen, and who you become will never be entirely under your control. But those are not good reason to evade questions of identity, when considering the impact of your choices.

Trap 3: Practical Misfocus

Because the most immediate impact of events that trigger the first transition is practical, I found that couples focused on finding practical solutions. They translated the question, "How do we make this work?" into the question, "What should we do?" This focus is understandable, but it traps couples and prolongs their struggle.

A useful metaphor here is that of the iceberg. When navigating through Arctic waters, mariners encounter many icebergs. The visible tips of the icebergs are hazardous and must be avoided.

What lies beneath the surface, however, is not only more danger-ous but also drives the movements of the part above the water. Unless mariners pay careful attention to what is below the sur-face, they will be on a collision course.

Practicalities are the tip of the iceberg for two-career couples. Because people can clearly see them, feel the pain they cause, and know they need to navigate around them, they all too easily ignore what lies beneath. And as much as you wish there wasn't, there is always something lurking beneath the surface of the prac-tical aspects of life. Struggles for power and control, unhelpful ways of relating to each other, assumptions about how your part-ner should behave or what a relationship should be like, your own hang-ups, your hopes and dreams—all these psychological and social forces contribute to the challenges you encounter and the choices you make.

Consider the story of Alejandro and Jasmine, whom we met in chapter 2. Their first transition was triggered by Jasmine getting a promotion opportunity in Vancouver, twenty-seven hundred miles from their home in Toronto. They agreed that living apart was not an option, and we left them wondering whether they should both move to Vancouver, let Jasmine pass on the promo-tion, or look for a third way. Like many couples, Alejandro and Jasmine approached their decision from a practical standpoint. They reasoned that as Jasmine's opportunity was a promotion, if Alejandro could find a position in Vancouver that was similar to, or better than, the one he held in Toronto, then they should move. The economy was buoyant, and Alejandro easily found such a position there, equivalent to if not slightly better than his prior job. They moved across the country six months before their wedding and started a new life.

Initially, all seemed well. The wedding preparations, the big day itself, and the honeymoon carried them through the first nine months. But once life quieted down, cracks began to surface in their relationship. Alejandro felt a nagging resentment that he had been the one to follow Jasmine's career. Ashamed of his feelings, he tried to push them away, but the harder he pushed, the more unsettled he became. On her part, Jasmine sensed that she had, as she put it, "upset the natural order." Without consciously realizing it, she took steps to correct the balance. She became overly accommodating at home, insisting that Alejandro make all the decisions, from what to eat for dinner, to which apartment they should live in, to what they should do on the weekends. At the same time, she resented being pushed into the role of submissive wife.

Neither of them was happy with the direction their relationship was taking. Both knew its downward spiral had begun with the move to Vancouver, but neither could figure out why. They kept coming back to the decision to move, but each time they reviewed it, they did so from a practical perspective and confirmed the decision's rationality. So why was it not working?

Like many couples, Alejandro and Jasmine were committed to equality, but were raised in families and a society that bombarded them with messages that men should be the career leaders and should set the balance of power in a couple. Many couples only realize how much conventional values hold them hostage when they make a decision that defies them. In this situation, the values pop up and create conflict and anxiety.

To manage this conflict, couples often make compensatory moves—such as Jasmine's overaccommodation—to conform to social standards even in their nonconformity, especially at home. Research shows, for example, that women who earn more than their husbands do proportionally much more housework than their husbands, and significantly more than women who earn less than their husbands.[11] These compensatory moves are unconscious efforts to reassert traditional gender roles and rebalance the power dynamic. However, when couples make these moves without realizing what is driving them, they often increase their anxiety and create confusion.

In their rush to solve the practical issue of where they should live, Alejandro and Jasmine had not taken time to explore how they really felt about Alejandro following Jasmine's career opportunities, nor how they would manage the shifting power balance in their partnership. Returning to the iceberg metaphor, Alejandro and Jasmine had focused solely on what was above the surface and not what was underneath. In not considering them up front, these under-the-iceberg dynamics hampered the success of their surface-level practical solution. They littered their path with regrets and guilt.

What could Alejandro and Jasmine have done differently? Like any couple faced with a hard choice, a better way might have been to first spend time exploring the under-the-iceberg implications of their decision. Typical forces that get activated by hard choices include power relations, assumptions about what a relationship should be like, and unspoken ambitions, hopes, and fears. Bringing these unspoken sentiments to light does not necessarily mean you should make your decisions to avoid experiencing them. If Alejandro and Jasmine had satisfied their lurking traditional values and not moved to Vancouver, it would have undermined their espoused egalitarian values, creating a different—and likely more problematic—set of issues. What discussing and bringing hidden forces to light does is ensure they are less likely to hold you hostage.

When you understand, share, and discuss the emotions, values, and fears underlying a decision alongside the practical aspects of that decision, it helps you to mitigate them in advance. Like all couples who fall into the trap of practical focus, Alejandro and Jasmine's initial response to their challenge temporarily solved the defining question of the first transition—"How can we make this work?" This solution, however, was a surface one, and their torment continued after their move was settled.

Trap 4: Doing It All

The final trap couples can fall into in their first transition is trying to do too much. This trap is set by the having-it-all assumption that many couples build in their honeymoon period. Together with the panic zone, it piles on the stress and makes it more likely that couples fall into one of the three decision-making traps detailed above.

In the honeymoon period, having it all can feel both realistic and desirable. However, as life gets more complicated, couples translate this aspiration into a do-it-all dictate that haunts them through their struggle period and beyond. If you want to have a great career, and a growing family, and a full social life, and hobbies, and couple time, and, and, and . . . it means that you will do an awful lot to keep all those balls in the air. When life gets more complicated, as it inevitably does when couples face their first transition, doing all these things simultaneously becomes a recipe for exhaustion, friction, and conflict.

Returning to Hannah and Santiago, whose story opened this chapter, their striving to do it all filled their life with activity while emptying it of intimacy. Their struggle was made worse because they weren't able to share their fears and instead plowed on until Santiago reached a breaking point. While Hannah and Santiago's situation may be unique, it doesn't take an international move and twins to fall into the do-it-all trap.

Claire and Joanna fell into this trap shortly after graduating from their MBA program. The two women had met at work in their mid-twenties and fell in love while on the same team in the company they joined after graduating from college. For three years, they enjoyed a full life—working hard, socializing, and enjoying the cultural opportunities living in a city had to offer. Then, driven by their career ambition and the choices their peers were making, they attended a local MBA program together. The program broadened their horizons and opened their eyes to the opportunities that a faster-paced career could offer. Both wanted more.

Upon graduation, Joanna took a job in a consulting firm and Claire in the mergers and acquisitions team of a bank. While both women's jobs were based in New York City, they spent most of the week on the road. Instead of relaxing on the weekends, their only time together, they rushed from one activity to the next, catching up with friends and hunting for an apartment to buy. The little time they spent together was so packed with doing that it eroded their intimacy. After six months, petty bickering morphed into serious conflicts. Realizing that their relationship was in danger, they pulled themselves back from the brink and put a halt to their frenzied weekends. A year later, though, they were slipping back into old habits. Doing had become a way of life that made it hard to just be, together.

The trap of doing it all is hard for couples to escape, especially for those who feel that they have the stamina and opportunity to do a lot, and should not let them go to waste. Even after the start of their first transition, many couples are still reluctant to challenge the assumption that they should try to have it all. Christoph and Eleanor were in their early fifties when I spoke to them. To their friends, family, and colleagues, they appeared a model couple, happy and successful; but privately, they were considering separating. We will hear their full story in chapter 8, but for now, and as a warning to those trying to do it all, take heed of Christoph's thoughts on how their relationship began to unravel:

> Looking back, I think if I could do things differently, I would have paid more attention to the ongoing nurturing of the relationship. There were some small, everyday things that I or we should have paid more attention to. Instead, we were always doing stuff. For example, we're very much into food and wine. We always bake our own bread, which takes time. Our children were brought up with homemade food in great variety. We put great effort into making healthy, homemade stuff, seldom buying pre-prepared food or using industrialized produce. Now that's fine in itself, but we did a hundred things like that. Frankly, I think we should probably have lowered our ambitions; nobody would have been harmed, and we could have spent more time talking to each other. Over the years, a distance built up to where we are now on the edge of breaking up.

With a focus on logistics, couples may be able to continue doing it all for a while, but, as Christoph and Eleanor's story shows, and as we will see in chapter 4, this external focus eventually comes back to bite.

Logistics Survival Strategies

Whatever triggers you face, you'll need to be mindful of the four traps that threaten your transition to a joint path on which you can both thrive. Even if you do it successfully, you will always have to deal with logistics. Every couple, young or old, wealthy or poor, faces a set of practical tasks they need to get done, be it managing finances, mowing the lawn, arranging a social life, or caring for elderly relatives. Traditionally, the lion's share of this work was done by a wife who did not have a job outside the home. Today's dual-career couples face the challenge of agreeing how to divide up this traditional "wife" role between them.

When couples in their twenties and thirties are in their honeymoon period, they often have few responsibilities and relatively straightforward lives. During this period, their logistical load is light and rarely a point of friction. Once they encounter their first transition, however, the logistics burden tends to increase. As life get more complicated, and couples' lives become more intertwined, there are simply more things to do. How you manage and divide up this logistics burden can be an ongoing source of conflict.

Let's return to Haru and Sana, whom we met in chapter 2. The arrival of their baby created a whole new world of logistics. Not only were there day-care drop-offs and pick-ups, there was also a constant mountain of washing, baby food to be made, trips to the doctor's, clothes to be bought, the house to be constantly cleaned, and the hundreds of other tasks new parents battle with. Before becoming parents, Haru had pitched in at home. But once Sana took her maternity leave, things changed. Like many new mothers, Sana picked up the lion's share of the logistics during her maternity leave and never let them go when she returned to work. As she and Haru quickly discovered, this division of work most commonly adopted by traditional couples simply doesn't work for dual-career couples. A wife doing close to 100 percent of the logistics load and maintaining a career leads to resentments and frustrations that push couples to the point of breaking up.

If a traditional logistics arrangement, where one partner does 80 percent or more of the household work, is not a solution for dual-career couples, then what is the best way to split these tasks? Recently, the idea of a 50:50 marriage, in which couples strive to divide all tasks equally, has caught our collective imagination.[12] While a noble ideal, I have found that couples who negotiate logistics well—that is, they are happy with the division of labor, do not resent each other, and can still push forward in their careers—are those who divide tasks deliberately, not necessarily equally. Here is a process you can follow to get to a deliberate division of labor that fits your couple's needs rather than a formula.

List All Your Logistics Tasks

Research shows that men and women consistently overestimate the proportion of housework they do.[13] Women believe they do the lion's share, while men believe the split is 50:50. In reality, the average man does sixteen hours a week of unpaid housework, while the average woman does twenty-six hours a week.[14] Clearly this isn't 50:50, but neither is it 90:10. A large piece of the discrepancy in estimations stems from simply not knowing what our partners do, and vice versa.

Just because you know that you—only and always you—water the plants, prepare the kids' gym bag, file the bills, or clean out the gutters, it doesn't mean that your partner knows it. In fact, as Tiffany Dufu explains in her book *Dropping the Ball*, we tend to be blind to household jobs that we don't do.[15] This not knowing leads to feelings of resentment and being undervalued. Starting your logistics strategy by jointly writing down a full list of household tasks is vital to avoid this trap of not knowing. This will ensure you are dealing with 100 percent of your tasks and nothing gets overlooked.

What Can We Simply Stop Doing?

With a having-it-all script running on overdrive, you are almost certainly doing some things because you think you should do them, rather than because you really need or want to. Does your house need to be perfectly tidy all the time? Do you need to bring homemade cakes for the school bake sale every time? Do you need to be the one who organizes all the get-togethers for your extended family?

Once you have your list of logistics tasks, it is tempting to dive straight into dividing them. Before you do that, take a hard look at your list and ask, "What can we stop doing?'" Sometimes we do things because it is expected of us in our community or, perhaps more accurately, because it is what we imagine is expected of us. Sometimes we repeat tasks we witnessed our parents doing or see what our current circle of friends focus on. Deliberately thinking through what you can drop will immediately take some pressure off your logistics burden and start to move you away from the trap of doing it all.

Which Tasks Do I Want to Own?

Logistics can get a bad rap. It is presented as a burden and carrying out tasks a sacrifice, but family duties are not all dull and onerous. Most of us take pleasure in and derive meaning from some of them. Before you think about what to outsource and divide, it is important to recognize what you personally want to keep. Perhaps you are a budding chef and love preparing family meals, maybe gardening is your thing, or you relish the kids' nightly bedtime routine.

One of the most successful couples I spoke to during my research—she the CEO of a nonprofit organization, and her husband a partner in a law firm—are a case in point. Both had extremely busy jobs, to which they were 100 percent committed; their four children had left home; and they had enough money to cover any logistical task they chose. Yet every Sunday evening she settled down to iron his shirts for the week ahead. As someone who hates ironing, I was bowled over when she revealed this ritual. "Why?" I asked, somewhat astonished, did she not get their housekeeper to do this?

"I love it," came her reply. "I've always done it. I find it relaxing, almost meditative. It's a way of expressing my love. It's actually a big piece of my identity as his wife."

Like this shirt-ironing CEO, often the things we hold dear are expressions of who we are as a husband or wife, father or mother. Recognizing them as such and claiming them is an important starting point. Of course, once you do this, there is likely to still be a lot left on your list, so for everything else . . .

What Can We Outsource?

Being in a dual-career couple does not automatically make you wealthy, but with two salaries, there is usually a little extra money to outsource tasks you really dislike or that take disproportionate amounts of time. Whether its ironing, cleaning, gardening, or grocery shopping, outsourcing some tasks frees up your time to focus on the things you really value. Some couples disagree on what or how much family logistics to outsource. Whom to outsource child care to, and for how many hours a week, can be an emotion-filled decision, and one that we'll explore in detail in chapter 4. For everything non-child-care related, go back to your list of tasks, identify your least favorite, your weekly budget, and then outsource as many as possible within your means.

When you are facing a particularly busy or stressful period—a big project at work, the run-up to a promotion, the arrival of a new baby—it is important to revisit your outsourcing arrangements. Getting a bit of extra help during these times, even with things you wouldn't normally, can make the difference between managing and burnout.

How Can We Split the Rest?

Once you have dropped the unnecessary tasks from your list, claimed the things you love, and outsourced some of your least favorite, you are left to split up the rest. While there is no one-size-fits-all solution to splitting tasks, the way you go about it can make the difference between relationship harmony and conflict.

There are two main strategies. The first is division, where you divide the tasks and each of you takes responsibility for those assigned to you. Some couples choose to divide the tasks equally, while others assign proportionally more tasks to one partner who perhaps has a less demanding career or a greater desire to get things done. The second strategy is turn-taking. Here you share responsibility for each task, taking turns as to who does what. Your respective turns may correspond to days of the week when you are relatively less busy with work. For example, one of you cooks dinner on Monday through Thursday and the other on Friday and over the weekend. Whatever you pick, the key is clarity. Tensions almost always stem from a lack of clarity, rather than a lack of equity.

Struggling to Do It All

The struggle is the most difficult period of any transition, and not all couples make it through. Caught by one or more of the four traps, they can find themselves at dead ends from which they cannot escape. Even if they survive, couples describe this period as an emotional roller coaster. Staying together through the struggle, however, is not enough for couples to successfully complete the first transition. Couples must find an answer to the question, "How can we make this work?" The struggle teaches them that the answer cannot be found at the practical level and requires a deeper accommodation in their relationship that takes into account values, beliefs, and feelings. When couples surface all of those, they can deliberately accommodate to the life event they face.

4

Achieving Interdependence

The warm evening breeze rustled the skirt of Emily's summer dress as she sat down to dinner with Jamal at Sonora Grill, their favorite restaurant in Mexico City. Their server lit a candle and handed them menus. "The perfect evening for a romantic dinner," he said with a smile. Emily and Jamal responded with wan smiles of their own. Romance was not at the top of their minds. After eighteen months of struggle and painful marital conflict, they desperately needed to find a path forward. They were hoping that a relaxing evening together might somehow help them break the impasse.

For Emily, it was only a hope. But Jamal had a plan.

After the server had delivered two mojitos and taken their dinner orders, Jamal reached into the bag he had brought. He pulled out a folded sheet of paper and a handful of colored pens. Pushing aside the silverware, the candle, and a small vase of flowers, he spread out a photocopied map of North America and handed Emily a green marker.

"We can't go on making career trade-offs," he declared. "We need to find a place where we can *both* thrive."

Four years earlier, when Emily and Jamal had first met in Houston, trade-offs were the last thing on their minds. In their late twenties, they were high-energy, optimistic, and determined to live life to the fullest. A project manager in a civil engineering firm, Jamal traveled extensively for work and often whisked Emily away to join him for impromptu weekends of wilderness hiking—a shared passion. These exhilarating getaways made up for the separate lives they led during the week, with Jamal traveling and Emily working hard at her job as a procurement specialist in a clothing company.

Eighteen months after their first date, they married in front of an intimate group of family and friends in Emily's hometown of Rochester, New York. After a honeymoon trekking in the Rockies, they moved into a small apartment with a view of the Buffalo Bayou River, and their lives continued much as before. Emily was promoted to her first management role, Jamal was given more complex projects to lead, and they both seemed to thrive.

Then, in the space of three months, their world turned upside down.

Two months before their first child was due, Jamal was asked to run a critical infrastructure project in Mexico. Emily and Jamal had become accustomed to managing everything that came their way with relative ease, and they recognized this assignment as a great career opportunity. Jamal agreed to spend three weeks out of every month working in Mexico City. The additional money he would earn would more than pay for extra child care. This arrangement would allow Emily to keep working and let them both continue pursuing their careers in parallel—or so they believed.

But when Aisha was born two weeks earlier than expected, Jamal missed the birth, stuck in the Mexico City airport waiting for a flight home. Suddenly their lives began to spiral out of control. Single-handedly managing Aisha, her job, and their home in Houston, Emily discovered that "additional child care" fell short of what she needed to avoid impending burnout. Jamal was exhausted by the relentless travel and the stress of the giant new project. Emily felt overburdened and unappreciated; Jamal isolated, incompetent, and guilty. Both felt locked into the arrangement they had agreed to.

It all came to a head the weekend of Aisha's first birthday. It was Jamal's week in Houston, but the intimacy he and Emily had once enjoyed seemed unattainable. Instead, the tension that had been building for months boiled over into a series of arguments. On Sunday night, with Aisha crying and an Uber driver waiting downstairs to take Jamal to the airport, Jamal told Emily, "I can't take this much longer. If we don't fix this somehow, it's over between us." He then stalked out of the apartment, banging the door behind him. He cried the whole plane ride back to Mexico—whether in anger or sadness, he could not tell.

That moment forced Emily and Jamal to realize that "having it all" was no longer an option, and that maybe they would end up with little left of "it" other than the pieces of a once-passionate love. Being action-oriented, they spent their evenings the following week on the phone, debating possible solutions. Emily found that she could negotiate a nine-month project role with her employer that enabled her to work remotely. They sublet their Houston apartment and the young family reunited in Mexico City.

For the first few months, they enjoyed the expatriate life. They found a nanny whom Aisha loved, and they relished being able to enjoy their daughter together every weekend. But soon the cracks resurfaced.

Emily's career suffered. Feeling disconnected from her company's head office and passed over for promotion, she grew resentful of what she called the "sacrifices" she was making for Jamal. Meanwhile, Jamal's boss began talking about the next project—in a new location. What would Emily and Jamal do next? Would they return to Houston so Emily could revive her career? Or would Jamal's career trump Emily's, forcing them to migrate to another new home? The fights resumed, more intense than before.

That was the setup for their evening at Sonora Grill. "You have a green pen, I have this red one," Jamal said. "Let's start marking the map. Which country, states, and cities can you see yourself living and working in? Draw some circles around them. Which ones would you hate to be stuck in? Draw some X's through them. I'll do the same in red. By the time we're done, we'll have a map that will show us where we can live together."

Emily was a bit dubious. She wondered whether their problem could be solved so simply. But she loved Jamal, there was no question of it, and was willing to give his plan a try. She pulled the cap off the pen and began making green marks across the map.

The Independence Trap

I found that most stressed-out couples who are struggling with their first transition do so for an overarching reason—while together as a couple, they still treat their careers, commitments, and lives as fundamentally *independent*. Based on this assumption, they seek to make compromises that trade wins and losses. They try to balance a concession in one area by Partner A against one in another area by Partner B.

Compromises are not bad. All relationships require them. But trade-offs are not enough—because true life partners are not independent, but rather *interdependent*. This mutual dependence requires couples to collaborate rather than barter. They need to dig below practical day-to-day issues that can be temporarily resolved through trade-offs and address deeper questions of career prioritization and life structure.

As Emily and Jamal's story illustrates, embracing interdependence and tackling the questions it raises is not easy. It often takes a crucible to realize that trade-offs only take you so far. This is particularly true for those couples that live in cultures where independence is highly valued as the sign of being a successful, mature adult. Once they go down the "trading concessions" path, the relationship becomes an accounting exercise.

If you live in such a culture, you recognize the symptoms. You're bombarded by messages that tell you, "Stand on your own two feet," "Take charge of your life," and "Be your own person." These messages have a positive impact on many of us. There are times in life when everyone needs to be autonomous and self-sufficient. And many people find it liberating and exciting to embrace the value of independence, especially in early adulthood—the first real opportunity for most people to test the boundaries of their potential and see whether they can "make it" away from the parental home.

When I analyzed the stories of the couples I interviewed, I found that independence often continued to be a core value during the early days of their life partnership. Young couples usually have independent careers and few shared responsibilities; and new love, if anything, makes them feel freer. Problems arise when those shared responsibilities begin to emerge and love begins to make demands on their lives. Approaching the new challenges they face through the lens of independent, parallel lives, couples focus on practical issues and search for ways to continue maximizing their individual aspirations. At that stage, that is the deal in many dual-career couples: "I'll cherish your freedom, and you mine." The result is a zero-sum game—one partner's gain is the other's loss. This deal, in which there is inevitably a winner and a loser, breeds resentments and envy, putting couples on the fast track to breakup.

The independence trap leads couples to ignore the deeper forces that shape the practical issues they face—how their careers are prioritized and how they should craft a shared, interdependent path. As Jamal and Emily discovered, until couples address these underlying forces, the solutions they devise will be mere Band-Aids.

To resolve their first transition, couples must accommodate to the life event they face by deliberately negotiating how to prioritize their careers and divide family commitments in ways that respect each other's needs, fears, and dreams—and reflect the ones they share. Once they have done the work of deliberate accommodation, they can craft a joint path along which they will travel until they face their second transition.

Whose Career Takes Priority?
Three Models to Consider

Jamal and Emily learned the hard way that no couple can have it all. Tough choices must be made. But how should couples make those choices? If partners are offered jobs at opposite ends of the country, where should they move to? If both need to travel for work at the same time, who gets to go and who stays behind to take care of the kids? If one partner needs to invest a Herculean amount of time preparing for a promotion, must the other partner pick up the slack at home?

These dilemmas point to the same underlying issue: *Whose career takes priority?*

When you find yourself embroiled in battles over questions like those above, it's important to take a step back from the specific question and focus instead on the broader issue of career prioritization.

Taking a deep dive into that issue can help you agree on a model that makes sense for your couple. The model will serve as a template for evaluating options and addressing those dilemmas and many more. There are three basic options you may want to consider.

Primary-Secondary

In a *primary-secondary* model, one partner's career takes priority over the other's. The person with the primary career dedicates more time to their work and less to the family than their partner does. They take the lead in planning geographic moves, and their professional commitments—for travel, for social events, and for weekend and evening work—usually take priority over those of their partner. The partner with the secondary career usually takes the lead role in the family and home. They can still have a full and successful career, albeit usually at a slower pace than their partner's.

This model of career prioritization was adopted by most of the early dual-career couples who broke the ground for the rest of us in the 1970s. Back then, because of social customs and traditional assumptions, the man typically held the primary position and the woman the secondary position. Today, some couples still choose the primary-secondary model—but the gender split is less straightforward and one-sided.

The major benefit of the primary-secondary model is role clarity: each partner takes the lead in one domain—work or family—which makes many decisions reasonably simple. The danger of this model is that, once adopted, it can be hard to change. People tend to become invested in the role they have assumed, making it hard to switch roles when life circumstances or the preferences of a partner evolve. What's more, when one person has been in the primary position for several years, their earning potential may have far outstripped that of their partners, making a role reversal even more difficult.

Turn-Taking

In the *turn-taking* model, partners agree to take turns in the primary and secondary positions. On the surface, a turn-taking couple may appear to follow the primary-secondary model. The difference is that they periodically switch who is in the primary and who is in the secondary position. Typically, these switches occur every three to five years, although some couples commit to longer or shorter periods to adjust to specific career and personal circumstances.

The benefit of the turn-taking model lies in the fact that both partners get a shot at investing heavily in both their career and in their family. Research shows that both men and women have equally strong desires to spend time with their families, as well as an equally strong sense of guilt when they cannot do so.[1] Turn-taking gives partners some balance between career and family, a balance that is increasingly important to couples.

The downside of turn-taking is the ambiguity about when the tables will turn. Discussing the timetable in advance is helpful— but it can be hard to anticipate how careers will develop. What should a couple do if one partner is offered a big promotion six months before they are scheduled to shift into the secondary role? Such unexpected challenges can trigger a relationship crisis that is difficult to resolve.

Double-Primary

Partners in the *double-primary* model dynamically juggle *two* primary careers. Of course, this is difficult to do. The major strategy for accomplishing it is to set explicit boundaries that help the partners remain on an equal footing.

These boundaries may be physical; for example, the couple may agree to remain rooted in a particular city and refuse to consider a move, no matter which partner's career would be affected. They may be temporal; for example, the couple may set rules regarding a maximum amount of work-related travel time or weekend meetings, or rules designed to equalize the sharing of household tasks and child care.

The double-primary model is attractive because it is egalitarian. Both partners are on a more or less equal footing all the time, and both can invest in their careers and family simultaneously. The danger is that, unless couples set strong, clear boundaries and adhere to them faithfully, they can quickly fall into the trap of trying to do it all.

Which Model Is Best? The Surprising Answer

Perhaps the idea of selecting a career-prioritization model makes you uneasy. You may feel that a more spontaneous approach, in which decisions are made on an ad hoc basis as they become necessary, is more realistic and less rigid.

It's true that committing to a career-prioritization model forces you to constrain your future decisions, which will feel restrictive. On the other hand, decades of psychological research have shown that, paradoxically, having clear life boundaries tends to make people feel psychologically safe and therefore more likely to make choices that allow them to experiment and grow. Many other studies have shown—again, paradoxically—that having fewer options rather than more makes it easier for people to choose one and leads to greater long-term satisfaction with the choices made.[2]

So rather than simply rejecting the idea of a career-prioritization model, I urge you to consider it seriously and discuss it with your partner. If you decide to choose a model and live with it for a time, you have the option to change or discard it by mutual agreement. And even if you decide not to commit to a model, discussing the options and your feelings about them will be an eye-opening process that will help you learn more about your partner's values and desires—as well as your own.

You may be naturally drawn to one of these prioritization models—or strongly averse to one of them. Each has its pluses and minuses. But is one model more successful than the others in promoting long-term satisfaction and strong relationships?

Whenever I speak about my research on dual-career couples, I always ask audience members which career-prioritization model they think is most successful. There is usually a range of views, but most people say they have been told or read somewhere that the primary-secondary model is the best path to a happy life. When I ask why this might be so, people argue that, in this model, both partners have clear roles, leading to fewer conflicts and simpler choices regarding practical matters. Likewise, people tend to say that turn-taking is the least likely to work because of the confusion over when partners should switch roles.

That sounds logical enough. But my research reveals a different pattern. The most popular model among the couples who reported feeling most successful in their lives and careers was the double-primary model. Those couples were quick to mention the hard work that this model took, but they saw doing that work as a point of pride.

This discovery fascinated me. My first reaction was to think that their pride must have reflected the egalitarian nature of the double-primary model and the spirit of our times. As societies move toward greater equality, a more egalitarian model should produce greater satisfaction and success. But the variety of stories that couples told me, and the disparities between those on both the successful and unsuccessful ends of the spectrum, left me feeling that this explanation was too simplistic. I was convinced that there is no one-size-fits-all model of relationship success. Could it really be that one model of career prioritization was objectively better than the others?

To dig deeper, I looked at all the couples, regardless of their career-prioritization model, who reported feeling successful in their careers and their relationship. In searching for commonalities, I found that they shared one important thing—they had all explicitly discussed and agreed on how to prioritize their careers, rather than leaving the issue unexplored and unresolved. They were, once again, deliberate in addressing the question *How do we make this work?*

This finding explains why double-primary couples tend to enjoy greater success. By its very nature, the double-primary model requires couples to have open conversations and make explicit agreements about career prioritization. They must agree on boundaries, create their own definitions of fairness, and address specific areas of disagreement as they arise. So the double-primary model works in part because it forces couples to communicate more deliberately about career-prioritization issues.

Of course, the value of open communication in relationships is a truism—common sense, you might say. Yet in studying couples, it struck me just how many adopted or changed their models of career prioritization with minimal discussion.

Let's return to Cheryl and Mark, whom we met in chapters 2 and 3. Without prior agreement, Mark accepted a startup job requiring countless hours of work, forcing Cheryl to become the main caregiver for their newborn daughter while continuing to work full-time. In effect, they switched their model from double-primary to primary-secondary based on nothing more than an excited hospital bedside announcement. Cheryl anticipated the downsides of this choice. Why didn't she protest? And why do so many couples make career-prioritization choices in the same haphazard fashion?

Questions of career prioritization are deeply personal. They cut straight to some of life's most fundamental questions: *What do we want from life? What are our ambitions? What kind of life do we strive for as a couple? And who gets to decide?*

Such questions are about power, an issue that many couples, and perhaps most people, fear confronting openly, as the story of Ben and Lucinda illustrates.

———————

Recently married, Ben and Lucinda were renovating an apartment and considering when to have their first child. A medical devices sales representative, Ben typically traveled Monday through Thursday, while Lucinda, a product manager for a consumer goods company, rarely left the city. Although Lucinda longed for a child, she agonized over the life and career implications that the decision would entail.

"Right now," Lucinda told me, "our careers are on an equal footing. But I know that when we have a baby, I will have to take a step back. With Ben gone for most of the week, what else can I do?" She felt resentful that her career would have to slow down, and in her mind this was the only option.

By contrast, Ben was wholeheartedly excited about parenthood, feeling he had the "how to manage" question all figured out. He planned to transition from his sales representative role into a more static position in head office that would give him more time to be a hands-on dad. "There's no way I'm missing out on all the fun," Ben told me in a separate interview, "and I don't want Lucinda's career to suffer."

I was struck by the wildly differing visions Lucinda and Ben had of their future as parents. Wondering why they'd never compared notes, I realized they each held assumptions that stopped them discussing career prioritization. Lucinda was so sure that she would have to move to a secondary career position that she avoided the conversation to avoid having her fears confirmed. Meanwhile, Ben was convinced this was a nonissue, so why bring it up?

So the surprising answer to the question, *Which career-prioritization model is best?* is this: *Any* of the three models can lead to a successful and satisfying relationship—provided you discuss the options openly and explicitly with your partner and make a shared decision based on your real feelings, needs, fears, and desires. Then you won't be making trade-offs for the sake of your partner's career. You will be making sacrifices to have the life you crafted and to be the couple that you deliberately chose to become.

Parenting Models and the Gender Role Trap

Not all couples have children, but for those who do, another key element in embracing interdependence is finding a parenting model that both partners accept.

In the last fifteen years, the amount of time and energy parents have come to invest in their children has increased dramatically. In the mid-1990s, mothers spent an average of thirteen hours per week on child care, while fathers spent an average of about four. Today, mothers spend an average of eighteen hours per week on child care, while fathers spend an average of nine.[3] All the evidence suggests that this trend is driven both by social pressures and by personal choices. In other words, it's not just that society expects us to spend more and more time with our kids—we also don't want to miss their childhood.

What's more, feelings of guilt over not being able to spend even more time with one's children are so widespread that it seems clear that both men and women are conflicted about how to organize their lives with the well-being of their children in mind.

In fact, some dual-career parents I spoke to worried that their children were worse off than those who had a full-time, stay-at-home parent. They felt guilty that they could not attend every single school event; that they could not help with every homework project; and that someone else would sometimes take the lead role in caring for their children when they were sick. They worried that their failure to provide full-time parenting might somehow harm their children, leading to psychological or social dysfunction, poor performance in school, a sense of abandonment, or other problems.

Given the pressures exerted on parents by societal norms, these fears are understandable but have no basis in fact. A wealth of research has shown it. Developmental psychologists have tracked children over time—in some cases, for as long as fifteen years—measuring their cognitive skills, emotional development, social competence, ability to build and preserve relationships, and other traits. They have compared these measures among children with a full-time, stay-at-home parent and among those whose parents both work.

The results: no difference has been found between the development and well-being of children with stay-at-home parents and those with parents who both work.[4] What really matters is the quality of a child's attachments to their parents and other important adults.[5] When these attachments are strong and full of emotional intimacy, kids flourish, whether or not those adults have jobs outside the home.

If you still find it hard to shake off the feeling of guilt for being a working parent, remember that the guilt is overwhelmingly driven by culture. When I am in the United Kingdom (my home country) or the United States (where I frequently work), I hear many expressions of guilt from dual-career parents. In France (my adopted home country), such expressions are rare. The "failure" of dual-career parents is not a reality grounded in fact; it's a story we tell ourselves, and one we can choose to stop repeating.

So let's accept, without guilt, the basic realities of parenting. The fact is that all couples (dual-career or otherwise) outsource *some* child care—whether to relatives, a school or nursery, or a dedicated nanny. This is not simply a contemporary phenomenon. In many traditional societies, elder relatives in extended families do most of the child care while parents work. Outsourcing still leaves many hours of the week to spend with your children, and deciding how to spend those hours and how to share the responsibilities and the rewards of children has major implications for your relationship. As with career prioritization, it can be very helpful to make a conscious choice among alternative parenting models. Here are three to consider.

Lead Parent

In a *lead-parent* model, one partner takes the lead-parent role and bears most of the child-care responsibilities. This is not simply about time. It's also about holding in mind the whole system that surrounds and supports children—knowing what day sports practice is, when they need packed lunches for school trips, the vaccination schedule, the phone numbers of their best friend's parents, the names and alliances of the kids in class, the plan for carpooling to soccer matches, and so on. A close colleague of mine who has three sons likens her lead-parent role to being the family's central computer. While she splits most of the child-care activities with her husband, she is the one who is expected to know what happens when and how—and to deal with the unexpected whenever it happens, as it so frequently does. He "works" for her.

The advantage of the lead-parent model is its clarity. Not just the parents but also the children can find it simpler and more comfortable to know exactly who will be in charge of major parenting duties. And when the partner who serves as lead parent truly desires and enjoys the role, it can be very gratifying. The disadvantage, of course, is that the secondary parent may feel excluded from important moments in the life of the family; he or she may even end up with a burden of regret over "not having seen my children grow up."

Turn-Taking Lead Parents

As with turn-taking in career prioritization, this model calls on partners to take turns in managing the lead-parent role. In some cases, switches occur every three to five years, perhaps aligning with shifts between the primary and secondary career positions. In other cases, partners juggle the lead-parent role to accommodate shorter periods when one or the other is experiencing particularly intense demands at work. Just like the turn-taking model in career prioritization, the downside is that it can be difficult to negotiate when to swap positions.

Co-Parenting

In the *co-parenting* model, partners split the lead-parent role. They typically make this work by dividing the time invested in child-care activities as a roughly 50:50 investment and by sharing the "central computer" functions. For example, one partner might organize everything to do with sports, health care, and homework while the other organizes all the children's social and music activities and liaises with their teachers.

Key to the success of any parenting model is—you guessed it—that it is chosen deliberately by both parents, as well as that it complements their career-prioritization model as a couple. Obvious? Maybe, but many couples find the two out of kilter. Sometimes a couple's parental investment model has not caught up with a shift in career prioritization. More often, the mismatch is driven by gendered expectations. For instance, statistics show that on average, women invest more hours in child care than men—and this tends to be true even when couples explicitly agree on a co-parenting model and a double-primary career-prioritization model.

I frequently heard the stories of dual-career couples in which both partners were committed to co-parenting, in part because both wanted to be hands-on parents, and in part because neither wanted to pull back in their careers. Nonetheless, an imbalance between their roles was often apparent. One woman I spoke with, for example, explained that although her husband was a hands-on dad, both of them framed this as him being "helpful." She elaborated:

> On a Saturday morning over breakfast, he'll always ask "What can I do this weekend?" On the one hand, it's great that I get a lot more help from him than many of my friends get from their husbands. But that's the problem—it's *him* helping *me*. I'm apparently still the one in charge.

We could debate the cause of this gap between explicit roles and implicit ones, as many couples do. Perhaps some men simply sit back and expect women to run the parenting show; perhaps some women behave in ways that imply their desire to be in control. Perhaps it's a bit of both. The truth is that escaping traditional gender roles is very hard, even for couples with strong egalitarian values. Those traditional roles are encouraged and reinforced in hundreds of ways every day, from depictions in mass media to subtly biased assumptions built into personal interactions, such as when a schoolteacher automatically calls a student's mother to ask a question or arrange an activity.

The persistence of traditional gender roles helps to explain the fact that women spend more time than men on child care and housekeeping even when they are the principal breadwinners in the family. Clearly, we still have a long way to go to fairly balance men and women's input to the family, even in the most egalitarian societies. So be warned: though you and your partner may commit in good faith to a co-parenting model, the trap of traditional gender roles is likely to exert a powerful, continuing influence on your behavior, whether you realize it or not.

Making Choices Together: An Approach That Works

Achieving interdependence and avoiding the independence trap requires you to make choices. Making those choices deliberately means that you might say goodbye to your cherished independence, but not to your freedom. To do so, couples need to decide together which career-prioritization and parenting models work best for them, and then apply those models to the daily decisions that impact the quality of their lives. There is great satisfaction, and a sense of freedom and agency, in knowing that we have made our choices and we are living up to them, whatever those choices are.

It is, of course, easier said than done. Deciding whose career should take priority and which partner will devote more time and energy to caring for children are deeply emotional questions that cannot be answered rationally by listing pros and cons on a spreadsheet. So how can you talk about it in a way that will generate decisions you both feel ownership of and can live with happily at least for a time?

A good place to start is by discussing what you both want from your careers and life over the medium term—say, the next five years. Sharing career-prioritization and parenting models will help you get to the nitty-gritty of how it will all work.

Few people are completely clear on how they want every aspect of their love and working lives to work. Some of your aspirations may be fuzzy. And what works for you will always evolve over time. But if you focus on the next five years, you can probably come up with a fairly accurate list of goals you are aiming for and experiences you would like to have in your career and life. The following questions may help you draft that list.

- *Do you have one or more specific career goals?* Your goals may include some that are quite concrete—for example: "To be promoted to a management position," "To launch my own freelance business with at least three clients," or "To complete the training needed to earn a new certification in my profession." Other goals describe experiences you would like to have—for example, "To be assigned to jobs where I'll keep learning," "To take on projects that will hone my leadership skills," or "To do work that I find rewarding and contributes something of value to my local community."

- *How ambitious are you?* Over the next five years, are you trying to lay the foundation for a career that you hope will take you to the highest level of your profession, however you define that? Are you seeking to maintain your current level of success, prestige, power, and income? Or would you identify your long-term ambitions somewhere in between those two extremes?

- *What parental role would you prefer, if any?* If you have children or plan to have them, how would you like to be a parent? Which aspects of parenting are most important to you? What role do you hope your partner will take?

- *What aspects of your relationship with your partner are important to you?* Are there specific activities you want to be sure to include time and resources for in your life plan? These could include travel, sports, hobbies, cultural or artistic pursuits, community activities, and more.

- *What other aspects of life are important to you?* Is there a country, region, or city you want to live in, or don't want to leave? Are there leisure-time, health-related, cultural, social, or spiritual activities you want to begin or maintain? Which relationships with family and friends are most meaningful to you? Is there an educational program you'd like to pursue? Do you have a non-work-related aspiration that you'd like to achieve before you die—for example, to write a book, to climb Kilimanjaro, to sing in a choir, to master French cooking? How might these desires help to shape your next five years?

Try to devote a day or more to an open-ended conversation with your partner about these topics. If you can clear your busy calendars for a full weekend of such talk, so much the better! In the process, you're likely to learn a great deal about your partner and yourself—and maybe even to rediscover some of the qualities that made your relationship so exciting and liberating when you first met.

Once you have a good idea what goals you and your partner are aiming for, you need to figure out how to plan your lives in a way that enables you both to thrive. Expect to compromise—it's an almost inevitable aspect of our lives together. The goal is to come up with a plan that, over the short-to-medium term, will get each of you most of what you want, and will get both of you a sense that you are doing it the way you want it.

Most couples find that the toughest piece of the puzzle is choosing a career-prioritization model and then defining how to implement it. For example, if you agree to try the turn-taking model, who will have the primary role first? For how long? What career milestone will mark the point at which the primary and secondary roles should flip—a particular promotion, a specific annual salary, or some other accomplishment?

The Power of Career Mapping

One exercise that can be helpful in choosing your career-prioritization model is to draw your expected career trajectories. Consider role models whose careers you might hope to emulate and think about the turning points they experienced in their careers. From these maps, you may be able to extrapolate a pattern that your career may follow. Some professions, including medicine, academia, and the law, require long, modestly paid apprenticeships before taking off. Other careers, such as corporate jobs in large multinationals, necessitate geographic relocations to get ahead. Some careers accommodate periods of pushing ahead at full steam, interspersed with periods of slower growth, while others feel more like a full-speed-ahead race all the way. Still other careers, like those of serial entrepreneurs, involve cycles of exploration, growth, maturity, and departure that may be repeated three, four, five, or more times.

Map the career trajectories that you and your partner aspire to. Then compare the trajectories. The similarities and differences—and the varying patterns of highs and lows, income growth and stagnation, periods of high pressure and low pressure—can help you anticipate some of the most notable challenges and opportunities you're likely to encounter. It can also help you develop some creative solutions about how to prioritize your careers in ways that will be most satisfying and rewarding for you both.

———————

Alison and David met when Alison was in her final year of medical school and about to embark on a five-year oncology residency with relatively modest pay. David, on the other hand, had already been working for ten years as a general manager in a nationwide manufacturing company, and he was rising steadily through the ranks. Talking through the career patterns they were likely to face helped them figure out how to make their careers work together in a way they both found desirable. They knew that, for the next five years, Alison would need to work long hours every week, but that she would have a choice of geographic locations, since oncology residencies are available at many teaching hospitals around the country. Meanwhile, David's fast-track corporate career would require relocations every few years, probably initiated by the company with relatively little control for him.

Based on these expectations, they decided that, for the period of Alison's residency, David's career would be primary. He would accept assignments wherever his company sent him, and Alison would find a residency within reasonable reach of his work. In five years, when Alison would be close to graduation, the primary-secondary roles would flip. Alison would need to have her pick of locations to achieve her dream of becoming an oncologist in a university hospital. Mapping the likely inflection points helped Alison and David see that a turn-taking model would work best for them.

Mapping your careers can also help you anticipate traps around the corner. Once you've made tentative choices of a career-prioritization model—and a parenting model, if relevant—use your map to project yourself into the future. Consider these questions:

- How might we feel about the career and parenting choices we have made in one year? In three years? In five years?

- When we look back on the choices we are making today from the vantage points of the future, can we anticipate that there are career doors we have closed that we might wish had remained open? How will we answer this question in one year? In three years? In five years?

- When we think about our family lives, are there choices we are making today that we might regret in the future? How will we answer this question in one year? In three years? In five years?

Every choice we make has its risks and its downsides. But these reflections may help you to reshape your choices and lessen some of the most serious risks—regrets that come from acquiescing to one partner's decisions, or not making any decisions. For example, suppose that you opt for a primary-secondary career-prioritization model. Are there steps you can take to ensure that the career of the person in the secondary position does not slow down to such an extent that it would be difficult to switch to a double-primary or turn-taking agreement? Similarly, if you choose to commit to co-parenting, can you agree on steps you'll take to reduce the tendency to slide from true egalitarianism into traditional, one-sided gender roles?

Mapping the likely future paths of your careers and then revisiting those expectations from time to time will not let you control the future, of course. It will only help ensure that the choices you make in the face of life's events bring you closer to a future that works for both of you. Having a map will also help you realize when it's time to move to a different territory, reconsider those choices, and possibly change them.

Achieving Interdependence

When a couple finds their way out of the struggle of the first transition, they achieve *interdependence*. Both partners accept that they are mutually dependent—that they must rely on one another to fulfill their shared responsibilities, to accommodate the life events they face, and to achieve their aspirations. It doesn't mean that the duties, rights, and powers of the two partners must be identical—or that their lives are completely merged, and they must both pursue the same goals or prioritize their career and aspirations in the same way. But it does mean they are committed to working together to ensure that both are choosing, and both can thrive. And they recognize and honor the role each partner plays in the success and failure of the other.

It's not easy for couples to achieve interdependence. They must dig below the surface of practical issues—*Which work conference will we attend next weekend? Whose turn is it to pick up our daughter from day care?*—and tackle deeper questions related to career and life. If you can do this deliberately, you can chart a path out of the first transition and enjoy a period of shared growth before your second transition begins.

How Can We Make This Work?

NATURE OF THE TRANSITION

Moving from having parallel, independent careers and lives to having interdependent ones.

TRIGGERS

The first major life event a couple faces together. Examples include a geographic relocation, a major career opportunity, a serious illness, the arrival of a new baby, a decision to join two families from previous marriages.

DEFINING QUESTION

How can we make this work?

Couples must figure out how they can structure their lives to accommodate the life event they face and allow both partners to thrive in love and in work.

TRAPS

Overrelying on economic decision criteria

Overlooking the long-term consequences of decisions

Overfocusing on practical challenges

Doing too much

RESOLUTION

Deliberate accommodation to the major life event by agreeing on how to prioritize their careers and divide family commitments. Crafting a joint path along which they can travel until their second transition.

TOOLS

Couple contracting: Chart out your values, boundaries, and fears to help you craft a joint path (chapter 2)

Logistics survival strategies: Mindfully tackle the division of logistics to ease tension and conflict (chapter 3)

Career mapping: Forecast the shapes of your careers to help decide a career-prioritization model (chapter 4)

REFLECTIONS

How to talk: Tips on how to avoid communications pitfalls and encourage kindness—the most important predictor of relationship satisfaction (chapter 2)

How to make choices together: Questions to reflect on that will enable better decision making (chapter 4)

What Do We Really Want?

5

Hitting the Wall

It all started with a dream," Matthew told me. "I dreamed I was in one of my favorite restaurants with my boss, and he ordered two chocolate desserts for us. The dessert looked delicious, but I really didn't want it. I just couldn't take it from him."

Matthew was forty-two. Until that point, his life had been a ride on what he called the "success train." That is, he had achieved a lot professionally, but other than having chosen the destination and his travel companion, most of the time he felt like a passenger. Matthew had graduated from college and then earned a master's degree in international management. That was where he met James. Both were serious students and ambitious for their careers. They cherished their similarities, and it did not take long for them to fall in love and begin planning a life together. For eighteen years, they'd steadily risen through the ranks, Matthew in health care and James in the construction industry. They had sailed through the first transition, making a shared home and life that felt their own.

Since then, they had become the picture of success—a pair of tall, handsome young executives, committed to work and beloved by their colleagues.

So why was Matthew so disturbed by that dream?

He felt that it symbolized something fundamental about his life, he told me. The opportunities he was being offered looked appealing, but they were too rich, and he would regret indulging later. They didn't provide him with happiness or meaning. The dream gave an image to a torrent of feelings and questions: *What am I doing with my life? Should I have taken a different path?* Matthew knew he was fortunate and felt uneasy questioning the direction of his life. Yet the feelings of restlessness persisted. He began imagining an alternative path, one in which he abandoned his corporate career and explored less remunerative but more fulfilling possibilities.

Around this time, James was offered a big promotion to a senior management position in his firm. The role would involve more travel, but not a relocation. James was thrilled, but Matthew was distressed. Now his doubts felt like a betrayal. "James and I had this identity as the high-flying couple. Would he still love me if I changed direction?"

For the first time in their relationship, Matthew began hiding his feelings from James. James assumed that Matthew had cooled on their relationship. "We knew other couples who separated in their early forties," James told me. "I began to wonder if he still wanted to be with me. I even became paranoid that he might be having an affair."

After six months in this limbo of unspoken turmoil and unshared worries, Matthew and James took a short summer break on the coast. As they sat down for a meal of burger and fries on their first evening, James shot Matthew a searching look. He took a deep breath. "So. Are you going to tell me what's happening, or not?"

The Second Transition Begins

Fleeting doubts, troubling dreams, and nagging questions are all hallmarks of the start of the second transition. As couples enter their middle years, the stability of the joint path they crafted at the end of their first transition begins to crumble under a new set of challenges. Rather than wrestling with the life events that trigger their first transition, couples must now contend with existential questions and doubts about the foundation and direction of their lives. If the first transition requires owning one's choices, the second involves questioning those choices. And the more we own our choices, the harder questioning them is.

The questions seem to emerge out of thin air, creeping up on people to disrupt a well-functioning—and at times, apparently blissful—life. In reality, they have been brewing for years, accumulating outside people's awareness until they are substantial enough to be recognized. The questions often start small: *Is this the career I want? Where does my passion lie?* But they quickly expand into other aspects of life: *Is this the relationship I want? Am I who I want to be? What should I do with the rest of my life?*

The source of the questioning is simple: many couples I spoke to, having had the good fortune of a partnership and a career that worked for them, were on the receiving end, and put up with, a lot of demands. They had the resources and support to meet those demands in their careers and in their social lives, and to a great extent they felt that they had chosen to do so. But at some point, one of them started asking, "Why do I put up with this, and how long will I?"

I found that couples most frequently faced the questions that spark their second transition in their forties. At this stage, people have had enough professional and life experience to reflect on their success, recognize their limitations, and not want to waste their remaining potential. They also become less likely, if they have succeeded enough, to tolerate paying prices that seemed acceptable before. Whether positive or negative, their assessment sparks more questions. In a quote ascribed to Oscar Wilde, "The Gods have two ways of dealing harshly with us—the first is to deny us our dreams, and the second is to grant them." If you have achieved success and realized some dreams, you ask, "What was it all for? Is this all there is to life?" If you judge yourself to have slipped behind your peers, and failed to reach your dreams, you ask, "What will I do now?" and you face the disappointment of realizing that you may never accomplish your goals.

People's pressing need to author their lives as they reach their middle years has been so extensively documented that some psychologists consider it universal. Whether it is an intrinsic need, or simply the result of constraints posed by social systems on young people, is an issue for the philosophers. Practically, most people who have worked hard to secure career opportunities and social standing in their twenties and thirties, like the couples in my research, will feel the desire for more freedom from the very commitments they once longed to make as they hit their forties.

From Impasse to Individuation

Prior to our forties, whether we like to admit it or not, most of us follow a career and life path molded by social forces that take the shape of parents, friends, and peers at work. On graduating from college, we may apply to medical school and follow in our mother's or father's footsteps to become a family doctor. We may train to become engineers because that is what smart kids do in our culture. Unsure what first job to take, we may join a management consultancy or a bank because that signals talent and status to our peers. Not only do we do what is expected of us, we also become the person we are expected to be—the hardworking striver, the caring organizer, or the diligent follower. That our life paths and personae are initially shaped by others does not mean that we are weak or lacking self-awareness. It is a common pattern that, in the early years, serves many of us well, as anyone who has benefited from a demanding mentor will know. But its usefulness only lasts so long.

The internal questioning and doubts that typically emerge in people's forties are the first sign that their "true self" is tugging on the persona that they have developed to conform to social expectations. When the people I studied sensed, for the first time, that the life they were living might not be entirely their own, they often felt trapped. They knew that their current path could not continue. They wanted to recraft their path to reflect their own desires rather than what other people expected of them. But they were unsure what exactly their own desires were. They were stuck.

The developmental task of the second transition is to shift from adapting to social demands and expectations to identifying and pursuing what each partner wants out of their career and relationship. I call this task reciprocal individuation. The psychologist Carl Jung was the first to describe the process of individuation through which people craft a self and life rooted in their own unique interests and desires. Jung recognized that individuation was tumultuous, but he saw it as central to healthy human development. It is only through this process, Jung maintained, that we let go of our "ought to be" self, become the person we are meant to be, and follow a path that feels truly ours.[1]

I call the task of the second transition *reciprocal individuation* because to successfully pass through this transition, couples must be able to support each other's individuation and recraft their joint path to align with both of their interests and desires.

Many of the dual-career couples I spoke to for my research found this transition daunting and, like Matthew and James, initially avoided it. Matthew's fear that his individuation would betray his and James's "identity as the high-flying couple" illustrates the reason we avoid the second transition. Because, at least on the surface, the impulse to be more ourselves, the impulse to individuate, appears to threaten the very ability to be a couple.

Resisting the Second Transition

To enter the second transition and embrace the process of individuation, couples must accept that the joint path they crafted during their first transition is no longer fit for purpose. Doing so places a lot at stake. Their identity, relationship, and careers are all developed within and adapted to a life path that they must now call into question.

No wonder many couples resist: "I should count my blessings," "Life works, why rock the boat?" "I have too many responsibilities to indulge in self-doubt." I have heard couples tell themselves all these things and more in an attempt to quell their questioning. People's ambivalence about the second transition leads many to hesitate.

———————

Benjamin had been avoiding doubts about his career and life for almost a year when I first spoke to him. An IT security specialist, he had always been fascinated by computers and technology, and had sailed through a computer science degree and into a series of jobs in midsized companies. For the last year, however, he had felt increasingly restless and longed to explore other options. The thing that had attracted him to his career—solving other people's problems and protecting them from harm—had become a turnoff. He began to resent what he referred to as the "IT illiterates" he had to support. He was becoming weighed down by the personality clashes in the team he managed. But what else could he do? He repeatedly explained—more to himself than to me, I suspected—how it would be "impossible" for him to take stock and consider a different path forward. In his mind, he could afford neither the time nor the energy to do so.

Three years earlier, he had begun a relationship with Zoe, a laboratory analyst, following the breakdown of their respective first marriages. Both had children from their previous relationships; Benjamin had two girls who were seven and nine years old, and Zoe, a five-year old boy. And like many couples in second marriages, they juggled complex lives. Benjamin was deeply in love with Zoe. He admired her professional commitment and appreciated the openness of their relationship, something he had sorely lacked in his first marriage. He struggled, however, with their life arrangement.

Benjamin and Zoe rapidly went through their first transition from independent to interdependent lives. Zoe's son lived with them during the week and spent time with his father every other weekend. The opposite was true for Benjamin's daughters. Zoe and Benjamin had hardly any time alone. To make matters more complicated, Benjamin's parents, who lived nearby, were aging, and his mother had recently been diagnosed with Alzheimer's disease. Benjamin envisaged a period of heavy caretaking ahead. With all these responsibilities, how could he focus on himself?

Although Benjamin said that he valued the openness of his relationship with Zoe, he decided that it was best not to bother her with his self-doubts. Unsurprisingly he began to sense a growing distance between them, a worrying throwback to his first marriage. Zoe said that she felt the distance, too, when I spoke to her. Unaware of Benjamin's inner doubts, she assumed that he was cooling on their relationship. Able to sense these shifts, Benjamin convinced himself that his growing responsibilities and complex life meant that not sharing his doubts was the best course of action.

Benjamin is not alone. Couples' second transition begins during a time of heavy life responsibilities. In their forties, people are becoming more senior in their careers and may have a team of people depending on them; they are financially committed to mortgages, pension payments, and health care; and if they have children, they are responsible for their upbringing. The forties are also a time when some people take on the care of ailing parents. All these commitments can make the idea of investing in personal growth seem self-indulgent and the prospect of change risky. As a result, I found, many people denied their questions to themselves and their partners. However, as Benjamin and Zoe's, and Matthew and James's stories reveal, people may not explicitly acknowledge or share their turmoil, but their partners often sense it.

Rushing the Second Transition

While I found that some people resisted the second transition by avoiding their questioning and hanging on to their current life path, others rushed through their questions and jumped too quickly to a new path. Take Carla. At forty-three, she encountered the typical questions and doubts that trigger the second transition. She began to question whether her monotonous but time-intensive career in a design agency was really for her, and she longed to spend more time pursuing her passions. An action-oriented go-getter, Carla wasted no time in making a transition. She came home one evening and declared to her husband Francesco that she was going to resign and would be building a portfolio career involving a mix of freelancing design work that she had already begun to set up, as well as doing some voluntary work. A shocked Francesco grappled with the financial implications of Carla's move for the family, while she went out and built her new path.

Fast-forward nine months. Carla's restlessness had returned with a vengeance. No longer isolated to her career, Carla's questions focused on her whole approach to life. "I've always been running," she explained, "I don't even know why. What am I running toward, or away from? What do I want from life? I just don't know anymore." Carla felt confused that her transition had not put these questions to rest. She realized the pressure she had put Francesco under by thrusting him into the primary breadwinner position and was ashamed to admit that her move had made little difference to her inner world. She was also afraid. Would he support her in a second round of reorientation?

The mistake Carla made, and many others like her make, was to equate external change to a completed transition, to think that switching jobs was the sole answer to her questions. At their core, transitions are about our inner world. They require a new way of *being* in the world—a new approach to life, a new focus, and new priorities. For some people, this new way of *being* will lead to a new way of *doing*—a new career; a new interest; for some, even a new partner—but inner change must drive the outer one, lest the latter become a dramatic way to avoid the former.

Letting Go of the Old

All transitions start with an ending. In couples' first transition, they must let go of having independent careers and lives. In their second, they must let go of something more existential in nature. The inner questions people face signal that their self no longer identifies with the persona they have built to please others and the life path they have crafted to support it. The first step of this transition is to figure out what no longer fits. For Carla, it wasn't her job, but her "constant running." Your transition truly begins when you figure out and begin to let go of your way of being that no longer works—be it an approach to life, an attitude toward others, a worldview, or an assumption about how you should behave or for what you should strive.

I found that people identified what this way of being was when they dug beneath the things they were doing and looked at what was driving them. When Matthew, whose story opened this chapter, eventually dug beneath his discomfort with the "success train," he realized that he had crafted an inner world in which he constantly needed to overreach in order to feel good about himself. The habit of stretching himself confined him to a train that seemed to never stop, let alone allow him to get off. As he explained, "I had turned my whole life into a race for progress, not just at work. I strove to become the best cook possible, the fastest runner. It seeped into every aspect of my life." Once he realized it, Matthew described feeling a wave of sadness and loss: "I remembered the soulful little boy I once was, the boy who would sit in his parents' garden all afternoon drawing and reading. I wanted to get him back, to give him more space to be." Matthew's insight was that he needed to recapture a lost self and to do it, he needed to let go of, or at least diminish, the piece of him that relentlessly overreached.

Letting go of an old persona, an old way of being, is tough. While letting go frees the self to move on, it is also a death of sorts. It's an acknowledgment that the way of life that has got you *here* cannot get you *there*, and you probably don't yet know where *there* is. At this time, the tendency to think of *there* only in terms of external change holds people back. Your transition may well involve an external change, but it is the inner ending and the inner change that will lead you to the external ones. This makes your ability to stay with the inner questions and change critical.

Entering Liminality

It is only when people can let go of their old way of being that they can enter *liminality*—the central experience of the second transition. First described by folklorist Arnold van Gennep and later elaborated by anthropologist Victor Turner, liminality is the psychological state in which our identity is in suspension.[2] We are betwixt and between the old and the new. When people enter liminality, an opportunity arises to connect to layers of their self that are not accessible elsewhere. They no longer identify with their old persona, but they have not yet figured out their new way of being. In liminality, people do this figuring out; the self can just *be* because it is not yet defined.

Traditionally, liminality occurred between set roles and was marked by rites of passage. Adolescents would leave their tribe and be taken by elders to a physical liminal space to learn about their new identity as adults. Nowadays, when people enter the liminal world, they most often do so alone, without elders to guide their passage.[3] When people enter liminality, they board a boat with no charts and no idea what direction they should sail. In writing their charts and steering the course they have chosen, people become their own selves. In liminality, we become open to exploration and reflection—the fuel for individuation. The explorations we conduct, combined with deep reflections, allow us to unpick our choices and behaviors, make sense of our past, and feel our way into a new future. This shift does not occur through immediate realizations, but through a series of gradual revelations that together combine into a picture of what we really want and how we can go about getting it. It takes time.

Speed and productivity have become virtues in the modern world, but they are limitations when it comes to liminality. Just as an embryo needs its nine months in the womb to develop into a heathy baby, so do people need an extended period of time in liminality to develop a healthy individuated self. To overcome the pull of speed and productivity, you must enter liminality with acceptance—acceptance that the process will take time and acceptance that your most important tool is your ability to make sense of the experiences you have within liminality. As William Bridges, an expert on transitions, notes, "The way in [to liminality] is the way out."[4] When you can accept liminality and use it to build a deep understanding of who you are and who you want to become, you will naturally transition out of it and on to your individuated life path.

Reflection and Exploration

Reflection is one of the most important tasks in liminality. Reflection about the past—*What led you to your impasse? Who are you? Why did you make the choices you made?*—and reflection about your future—*Who do you want to become? What do you desire from life?* Reflection occurs in empty time. To reflect, you need to stop doing. Reflections can be purely in your own mind; they can also be made through journaling, drawing, or in conversations with others. Some people reflect alone. Long walks, time spent staring at the waves or at a roaring fire, afternoons pottering in the garden can all give us the calm and uninterrupted space in which our minds can wander and make associations. People can also reflect with others. Long conversations with friends, siblings, coaches, analysts, or our partners all give us a space in which we can share our thoughts and associations, drawings, and writings. Often the simple act of saying out loud what you think and feel helps to clarify your mind. Of course, many of us combine different ways to reflect, gradually feeling our way into what is most helpful.

I have found that couples who work well through their second transition include each other in their reflective spaces from the beginning. It does not mean that all their reflection is done together, nor does it mean that no one else is involved or they don't take time for themselves. What it means is that their thoughts and feelings unfold together, rather than one partner presenting their new life path to the other. They might be leaving an old life, but they take each other along to find a new one.

To reflect on the past, you need time. To reflect on the future, you also need data. This is where exploration—the other major task in liminality—comes in. Exploration gives us insight into the alternative selves we might become and the alternative paths we might choose to take. It involves engaging with new and unfamiliar worlds to gather information about the practicalities of an alternative path as well as understanding the kind of people who pursue it. This gives you a picture of both what you might *do* and who you might *be* if you take it. As my mentor Herminia Ibarra explains in her thought-provoking book *Working Identity*, exploration can take many forms.[5] One way is through structured networking events organized by alumni clubs or local professional networks. Such organizations hold regular gatherings that can be a great way to find out about different worlds. Other ways are more informal, such as asking friends, neighbors, and others in our community for introductions to people who have careers that interest you. Others involve less personal contact. There is a lot you can learn through reading books, articles, and blogs written by people in different walks of life. Others still involve active experimentation—job shadowing, secondments, or voluntary work to actually try out different roles. And of course, the best exploration combines all of these things to build as full a picture as possible of alternative paths.

Most career books are packed with great advice on how to explore alternative paths. What they pay less attention to is just how bewildering and anxiety-provoking liminality is. After eighteen months of running, Benjamin, the IT security expert we met earlier, finally admitted to himself and Zoe that he needed to stop being what he described as "the independent warrior always fighting my own battles and protecting everyone else in theirs." He had no idea what he should do with this realization. He only knew that he couldn't carry on with this way of being and that he needed to figure out who he wanted to become instead, and what he really wanted from life. Zoe was supportive of his exploration, but neither she nor Benjamin were prepared for the realities of his liminal experience. As he described it, "I was totally lost. I knew I couldn't go back, and at the same time I had no idea what forward meant. I spent a lot of time just thinking about how I had gotten here. I also went out and gathered information about other directions. I spoke to a lot of new people, but it took a long time for anything to become clear. Strangest of all, nothing had changed on the outside, I was still going to work, looking after the kids, caring for Mom, but I was somehow detached, there was a disconnect between what I was doing and how I was feeling, what I was thinking inside."

Benjamin's experience is common. While disorienting, liminality is ultimately a space of potential. It is the space in which we figure out what we want, the space in which we can explore the range of selves we may become and find a new direction. It is in this space that individuation occurs, and it is only by staying in it that you will figure out what you really want and who you want to become. The problem with the term *individuation* is that it can appear to be all about you as an "individual." It never is.

It's Never Just About You

When two people become a couple, they take a major role in each other's life story and, through the process of their first transition, they forge a joint interdependent path that connects two previously independent ones. Couples' focus in their first transition is on deliberately accommodating to major life events by negotiating how to prioritize their careers and divide family commitments in a way that suits them. Yet at the same time, I discovered through my research that couples implicitly negotiate the roles they will take in each other's lives. No couples I spoke to explicitly discussed these roles until they were in the midst of the second transition, but all established them early on.

If couples accommodated to their first major life event in a non-deliberate way—that is, if they fell into of one of the traps of the first transition and settled on a career prioritization and division of family commitments that didn't allow them both to thrive—they felt caught in their roles and regretted establishing them. If couples deliberately accommodated to their major life event, the roles they settled on initially served them well as they traveled along the joint path they crafted in their first transition. Over time, however, these roles—even when they were a by-product of a very deliberate accommodation—became constraining and were one of the sparks of the restlessness and questioning that led to the second transition.

The second transition is thus triggered by a combination of two forces—the drive to individuate that is part of the life cycle and the need to tackle the division of roles within a couple that is a consequence of the first transition. This combination of forces means that although couples are most likely to face the second transition in their middle years, I also found couples at other life stages who were wrestling through it.

In the three chapters that dealt with the first transition, we examined how agreements about career prioritization and family commitments let couples thrive (or not) in love and work. In this and chapters 6 and 7, we examine couples' deeper psychological agreements, which they need to surface and revisit to make it through the second transition.

Just as couples divide practical labor, they also divide psychological labor. Each partner takes on certain roles and relinquishes others. One partner becomes the expresser and holder of emotions, while the other becomes the rational planner. One partner becomes the energetic go-getter driving the family forward, while the other becomes the laid-back counterbalance. We gravitate toward roles that we have a personal affinity for, and as our partners relinquish those roles, we act them out for two and can therefore become exaggerated versions of ourselves. At the same time, we let go of sides of ourselves that our partner takes up on our behalf. Thus, partners in a couple can become polarized into consistently playing some roles and rarely playing others. The result is a division that makes us whole as a couple but incomplete as individuals.

When people reach the impasse that starts their second transition, the questions and doubts they face often point to a way of being that has been lost or underdeveloped, partly because during the first transition it was given to, and has since been lived out through, their partner. Carla, whom we met earlier in this chapter and who made a rushed transition from her design agency to freelancing, had always been a go-getter. But when she looked back, she realized that her "constant running" had been amplified by her relationship with Francesco. She had become the one who drove their family—not only was she the organizer-in-chief, she also kept things constantly running in her mind. She relied on Francesco to bring calm into their lives, to force her to take breaks, evenings off, or simply chill out. She admired his ability to switch off.

Carla knew that she used to be able to kick back too, though maybe not in the wholehearted way Francesco did. But when she looked back to her early twenties, she discovered a more care-free self. The polarization of roles in their relationship and her fast-paced career had let her go-getter self run wild and left her carefree self behind. Carla wanted to rebalance these two sides of herself; but to do so, she and Francesco would have to rebalance the two sides in their couple. Her individuation, in other words, required not only his cooperation and support, but also a change of his own.

Transitioning Together

Couples are like any kind of system—change in one part affects the rest. For one partner to change their way of being, the other partner has to adapt theirs. While people may say, and genuinely believe, that they support their partners' individuation, they support them exploring and becoming a new self with a new way of being and a new way of doing, they often resist it unconsciously. We are okay with our partner changing, as long as we don't have to give up being the one who holds all the emotions. We are OK with our partner becoming more ambitious as long as we don't have to hold in mind more of the practicalities. I found that the discomfort people felt about their partner changing was widespread. It signaled that they needed to change the roles they played in each other's stories. Seeing this as a negative evolution, though, is a mistake.

When your partner pushes back on the division roles in your couple, it presents you with a chance to reclaim lost or underdeveloped pieces of your own self, and to make both of you more psychologically whole. It is a developmental opportunity that can enrich a couple. Moreover, when one partner reaches their impasse, it often triggers an impasse for the other because partners emotionally resonate with what I call each other's developmental *stuckness*. Emotional resonance amplifies each partner's experience of stuckness and creates a joint impasse and a joint opportunity for change.

Three months after Benjamin confessed to Zoe the extent of his questioning and deadlock, Zoe herself began to share a similar experience. Unlike Benjamin, her doubting didn't concern her career, but the way she took up other roles in her life. As she explained, "I've always had other people looking after me. I'm still the little girl somehow. When I was a child, it was my dad who shepherded me through life. After college, I joined the lab and had a group of much older colleagues who treated me like their daughter." She went on to describe how her first marriage had followed a similar pattern until her then husband became emotionally abusive toward her following the birth of her son. "Benjamin saved me from that marriage and rebuilt my confidence," she explained. But she was back in the same pattern. For the first time in her life, the pattern felt constraining rather than comfortable. She longed to break out and stand on her own two feet. Soon, Benjamin and Zoe recognized a connection between their impasses—he was stuck in the role of the rescuer, and her of the victim. Rather than relieving them of these roles, their current psychological arrangements were cementing them.

As Benjamin and Zoe's story reveals, the impasse couples face at the start of their second transition does not signal that their psychological agreements are broken or flawed, but rather that the life path that those agreements supported is coming to an end, and to reorient to a new life path, they will need to renegotiate these psychological agreements. Couples, in short, must face the question, *What do we really want?*

What Do We Really Want?

Whatever form your internal questions and doubts take, they reveal the task of the second transition: to shift your focus from adapting to demands and expectations to identifying and pursuing what you each want out of your careers, lives, and relationship. Because this transition is in part about tackling the division of roles established in the first transition, it is not enough to ask, "What do I really want?" Your story is so intertwined with that of your partner that you must ask, "What do *we* really want?"

Just like the first transition, couples that work figure out the answer to this question together. Unlike the first transition, this figuring out will involve individual exploration interspersed with joint reflection. This exploration and reflection occur in the liminal world that we must embrace to make a fruitful transition.

In chapter 6, we will explore the traps that can ensnare couples as they meander through the liminal world and the struggle that accompanies it. We will focus on the support you need to give to, and receive from, your partner to make it through and the positive feedback loops that can emerge from mutually supportive behavior. Then, in chapter 7, we will address how couples can successfully craft a new life path once they have figured out what they really want and felt their way toward a new way of being.

The second transition is psychologically demanding, and not all couples make it through. This life stage is one of the peak times for breakups and divorce.[6] So before we move into the meat of the second transition, I'm sharing here some ideas for how you can bolster your *relational resilience* in preparation for the stormy ride ahead.

Relational Resilience

Resilient relationships endure, even in times of adversity. In chapter 2, we explored the importance of kindness and undivided attention in building a high-quality connection with your partner. The key to building resilience into this connection is your and your partner's mindset.

Psychologist Carol Dweck identified two types of mindsets—fixed and growth—that profoundly shape our motivation, success, and relationships.[7] People with a fixed mindset believe that intelligence, ability, and character are static traits that cannot be changed. In contrast, people with a growth mindset believe that those same qualities can be developed through dedication and effort. Research consistently points to the benefits of having a growth mindset, yet when it comes to relationships, people are bombarded with messages that reinforce a fixed one.

From an early age, most people are taught the narrative of relationships as destiny. The fairy tales that parents recount, the films people watch, and the magazine articles they read most often portray love as a quest to find "the one." While it may be romantic to believe that destiny brought you and your partner together, this belief hinders you from building relational resilience. The reason is that it fosters a fixed mindset.

When we have a fixed mindset, we interpret relationship difficulties as signals that we are incompatible with our partner. If we disagree or fight, we conclude that we are not meant to be together. When troubles and conflicts arise, people with fixed mindsets are more likely to disengage from their partner and withhold support.[8] Moreover, when bad times arrive, couples with a fixed mindset are less forgiving with each other, which, as we saw in chapter 2, can lead them to break up.[9]

In contrast, when people have a growth mindset, they believe that relationships grow when the couple works through rough times together. If partners disagree or fight with each other, they conclude that they need to invest more in their relationship. When troubles and conflicts arise, people with growth mindsets are more likely to stay positive, cope with the difficulties, and maintain a forgiving stance toward each other. In short, couples with a growth mindset are more resilient in tough times, and rather than weakening their relationship, difficulties can actually strengthen it.

So how can you and your partner foster a growth mindset, and in doing so, boost your relational resilience? Here are five ideas:

First, abandon the fairy tale image of "the one." Couples who have good relationships have them because they invest in each other, not because Cupid struck them with his arrow. Second, show gratitude for the effort your partner puts into your relationship. No one is perfect; everyone hurts their partner at times. What matters is your intent and investment over the long term. When you display gratitude for their efforts, your partner will respond by investing more.

Third, frame challenges not as wholly negative, but also as opportunities for growth. Relationships become resilient in tough times. You'll face plenty of these in your second transition, so embrace them as necessary and helpful. Fourth, value the process more than the result. How many times do you find yourself saying to your partner "When x happens, then we can relax/take a vacation/feel pleased with ourselves"? The problem is that one x is replaced by another, and it's through the process that you grow, not by reaching the destination. Take time to appreciate being in the muddle together.

Finally, celebrate your growth with each other. All too often, couples wait for external achievements to celebrate—the promotion, the pay rise, or the recognition. Celebrating growth in your couple, the overcoming of difficulties, the ease at which you can have meaningful conversations are important to keep your growth mindset alive.

6

Turmoil and Conflict

Chang paced around the kitchen, picking at leftover take-out. It was the second time in a week that Rose stayed out late at a networking event. Although he had been supportive of her attempts to change career direction, his patience was running out.

Six months earlier, Rose had surprised him with a call from her office. "I've just quit my job," she announced matter-of-factly. At first Chang was delighted. Rose's job had been pushing her close to burnout, and he was feeling the strain of supporting her. He assumed that after a few weeks of rest, she would be back on her feet and into a new job. As a skilled financial planner with devoted clients, Rose would surely be snapped up by a competitor. It hadn't turned out that way.

Rose decided that what she wanted wasn't simply a new job, but a new direction. Before she quit, she had entered "a death spiral," as she put it. What she was doing had become a turnoff, and she was fed up with her whole way of life. "I had become an uptight, rational automaton," she said, "I didn't like who I was. Realizing that was a huge blow, and at the same time it gave me a kick in the butt to change. I desperately needed to figure out what I wanted to do, and more fundamentally, who I wanted to be." While not literally suicidal, Rose wanted out of her life as it was. She could not take it anymore.

During the eight years before her "death spiral," Rose and Chang had enjoyed a relatively stable path. In their mid-thirties, they had tackled their first transition—a tough struggle to fit their careers together—but since then, minor family crises notwith-standing, they had both thrived in their jobs and relationship. Rose's impasse was an unexpected shock to their largely working system.

Quitting her job gave Rose some quiet time to reflect on her impasse. She used the time to read stacks of career books; driven by their advice, she plunged into a period of intensive networking. She discovered that she loved it. Forging connections with dif-ferent groups of people and exploring new career options made Rose feel more alive than she had in years. She relished sharing her adventures with Chang and telling him about the fascinating people she was getting to know.

Chang was happy to get back the outgoing woman he had fallen in love with, and initially feigned enthusiasm for her explo-rations. But as the days turned into weeks and the weeks turned into months, his resentment and jealousy grew. "Life revolves around Rose's existential crisis," Chang complained. "We were in a good groove before. I wish we could just rewind." Sensing Chang's lack of interest, Rose began to withdraw. She got plenty of support from her new contacts. Perhaps she didn't need as much from Chang.

It was 11:15 p.m. when Rose finally came through the door. She was beaming as she hung up her jacket and slipped off her high-heeled boots. "Hello, darling!" she cried. She'd stayed for drinks with two other women who were also in transition, and her mind was bubbling with thoughts of the camaraderie she shared with her "sister gang."

Rose was startled when Chang confronted her. "Who is he?" he asked abruptly.

Her smile disappeared. "What are you talking about?" she answered.

"It's obvious you're having an affair!" Chang snapped. "Just tell me who he is so we can stop pretending."

The Second Struggle

Faced with the internal questions and doubts that mark the start of their second transition, couples like Rose and Chang are thrown into the struggle period. The ground of the stable path they had crafted during their first transition begins to shift, and the belief that they had figured out how to make it all work falters. As both partners wrestle with their inner questions, their behavior, the roles they play in each other's lives, and their ways of relating change. This change is disorienting and threatening.

The disorientation and threat can lead to traps that intensify or prolong the struggle and curb the couple's ability to individuate. The first trap—mistrust and defensiveness—occurs when people are over-attached to their previous path and the role their partner played in it. The second trap—asymmetric support—occurs when partners lack the energy or will to support each other's transitions. Both traps make it difficult for couples to figure out what they really want.

How long couples spend in their struggle period, how severe the struggle becomes, and whether they can make it out depends on their ability to spot and avoid these traps. It also depends on their ability to genuinely support each other's transition.

Trap 1: Mistrust and Defensiveness

When your partner begins wrestling with who they are and who they wish to become, they will often, like Rose, go out and explore new life paths. This takes them away from your relationship and into new environments, where they meet new people and discover new passions. While exploration and reflection are essential fuels for growth, living with a partner who is absorbed in new pursuits can feel threatening.

Painful questions surface: *Why is my partner not satisfied? Is this a career or a relationship problem? Am I to blame? Why do they need new people? Am I no longer enough?* Like Chang, we can become suspicious of our partner's intentions, question their commitment, and fear their loyalty. These emotions lead us into the trap of mistrusting our partner and becoming defensive. When we act in this way, it pushes our partner to withdraw further from our relationship, which in turn makes us even more mistrustful and defensive, until eventually our relationship itself becomes an obstacle to, rather than a space for, individuation. In most cases, I found, people's suspicions and fears were grounded in fantasy, not reality, and in a self-centered view of their partner's struggle. Yet their reaction to those fears, an escalation of constraints and demands, did sometimes push someone's partner into the arms of another.

At forty-two, Avni felt stuck—stuck in a career that she was ambivalent about, stuck in a stagnant marriage, and most of all, stuck in her role as "the supporter." When she had married Sandeep twenty years previously, she admired his ambition and success. Six years her senior, he was rising quickly through the ranks of a global defense firm. In their early years, Sandeep encouraged her ambition. She spent the first four years of married life studying for a PhD in chemistry, followed by a three-year post-doctoral fellowship in the United Kingdom, where she had followed Sandeep with his work. After two sons arrived in quick succession, they moved home to Chennai, India, to be close to their families.

The geographic move, her new responsibilities as a mother, and her growing dissatisfaction with academia prompted Avni to switch to a career in business. On Sandeep's suggestion, she joined the human resources team of a large technology firm with offices close to their home. Although she enjoyed the tech environment, she disliked what she saw as the "background role" of HR. "We are never recognized in the business," she explained. "It's like at home: Sandeep is seen as the star and I'm praised for being the family foundation." As she entered her forties, she had had enough of being the supportive wife, supportive mother, and supportive HR professional. She was desperate for a change and wanted a chance to shine and to honor her own ambitions.

Avni took a three-month sabbatical to give herself time to think and scout opportunities. Sandeep was supportive at first, but as she began to explore different worlds, his backing waned. He became possessive, critical, and uninterested in her reflections. He put pressure on her to restart her job, trying to persuade her of its positive aspects. It was then that Avni met Vikash. Like Avni, Vikash was in the midst of a transition. Their common experience sparked a connection, and they began an affair. Describing her attraction to Vikash, Avni said, "He saw me in a way that Sandeep could not. He seemed genuinely interested in my thoughts, my feelings, and in who I wanted to be. For the first time in a long time, I felt seen as a whole person."

Avni's desire to be seen as a whole person is one that many people share. In times of transition—when we often feel as though we're in pieces we can't yet fit together—this desire is even stronger. Being witnessed gives us an anchor amid the turmoil. But as Avni discovered, it is not enough to sustain a relationship in the long term. Her affair with Vikash ran its course, and she and

Sandeep began the long road to rebuild their marriage. While he was devastated by her infidelity, Sandeep came to understand his role in it: "The other man gave her something that I didn't understand she needed. I had gotten so used to seeing Avni in the way I wanted to, that I had ignored what she really wanted. I regret that."

Keeping Our Partners Stuck

Whether you like to admit it or not, you are probably a lot like Sandeep, invested in seeing your partner in a certain way and reinforcing the role they play in your life. When the way you see your partner ossifies, you are more likely to fall into the first trap of the second transition—to experience their exploration as threatening and not trust their intentions. Furthermore, if you are unwilling to recraft the path you built during your first transition, the threat posed by your partner's attempts to individuate is not imagined, it's real. The vicious cycle that this threat sparks intensifies the struggle, brings strife to relationships, and makes the transition to an individuated life more difficult.

It is well documented that people need to engage in exploration and reflection to work through impasses and individuate. Browse through any of the books on career transitions, and you will find step-by-step guides on how to do so. The mystery is why, faced with this wealth of guidance, some people don't do it. Why, by their late forties, do some people still feel stuck in a life that is not theirs? Why do some people not craft an individuated life path? Does their relationship have something to do with it?

These are some of the questions I sought to answer in my first research project on dual-career couples, together with my colleague and friend Otilia Obodaru, a professor at the University of Bath.[1] We examined what differentiates couples in which both partners can figure out what they want and move to individu-ated life paths from couples in which one or both partners re-main stuck. We found that avoiding the first trap and accepting the other's need to explore was important, but alone it was not enough. The key, we found, was an important role partners can play for each other—the role of a secure base.

Secure Base Relationships

Psychologist John Bowlby, a pioneer in the field of child devel-opment, wrote that "all of us, from cradle to grave, are happiest when life is organized as a series of excursions, long or short, from the secure base provided by our attachment figures."[2] Bowlby was one of the founders of attachment theory, which describes how people's close relationships influence who they become and how they relate to others throughout life. He showed that people always need a secure base—someone who encourages them to explore and take risks, and at the same time gives them a safe place to retreat to between their challenges and adventures—to develop as individuals.[3]

At any age, people's personal development occurs through exploration: adventures away from their familiar comfort zones. Leaving one's comfort zone provokes anxiety and uncertainty. Having a secure base is the way we manage these feelings and manage to keep exploring and so keep growing. While most chil-dren look to their parents to be a secure base, most adults look to their partner to play this role.

When you are a secure base for your partner, you are depend-ably supportive and you encourage their exploratory behavior. In practice, this means two things. First, that you try to soothe your partner's anxiety associated with exploration and reflec-tion. To do so, you must acknowledge—without downplaying or exaggerating—their anxiety and be an open sounding board for them to share their emotions, highs and lows, fears and doubts. At the same time, you must encourage them to move away from the safety of your relationship to explore new worlds and engage with new people. This encouragement can feel like a loving kick. Through it, you do not allow your partner to wallow in self-pity or apathy, but rather urge them to go out into the world and figure out what it is that they want and how to go about getting it.

Putting the two sides of a secure base together can feel paradoxical. You must comfort *and* challenge, you must be close *and* push away. Yet these two sides do belong to one coin. When your partner depends on you to hold them, they are more likely to respond to your encouragement to move out of their comfort zone. Put another way, the more secure they feel in your relationship, the more easily they can move away from it.

The Power of Mutual Secure Base Relationships

I found that couples who make it through their second transition and recraft individuated paths are most likely to have mutual secure base relationships in which both partners play the role of secure base for each other. One such couple is Indira and Nick. After seventeen years together, two successful and balanced careers, and three children, Indira and Nick felt that they had figured out how to make life work for them. Then, as Indira hit forty, she began to feel restless in her corporate communications job. What began as a simple feeling of needing a job change quickly morphed into questions of identity and life choices that profoundly impacted her and Nick:

> As I turned forty, I started to feel conflicted. On the surface, my job was good. I led a small team and had a reasonable

budget, but I realized that something deeper underneath was bothering me. At that point, I felt very low. I took antidepressants for two months just to help me through. Eventually, my doctor signed me off work for six weeks of sick leave. I just couldn't do it anymore. That's when I realized I was just an object pursuing a career path that I hadn't really chosen. I didn't like the feel of my company, but I didn't understand why. I was really in an identity crisis.

Indira's crisis rocked the foundations of her and Nick's well-structured world. She withdrew from their once-vibrant social life, struggled to explain her absence from work to her children, and felt racked by guilt that she had let Nick down. She had prided herself on being a rock for her family; now she felt that the rock had crumbled. Her husband's support helped her through this low point:

> Nick got worried about me because he saw that I physically couldn't, I didn't want to do it anymore, so he was worried about my mental and physical health. I stayed home for a period, which Nick was very accepting of. I am forever grateful for that period, when he was just like, "Take the time you need, and then you'll see." He didn't accept me just sitting around feeling sorry for myself, though; he pushed me to look into different options and really think through what I wanted. In that time, I really invested in myself. I explored many different options, and all the time Nick was there to talk things through.

Nick gave Indira exactly what she needed to hold her troubling emotions and support her development—acceptance of her impasse, encouragement to explore options, and no pressure to make quick decisions. In being a secure base for Indira, he witnessed her journey, which in turn sparked his own. As he explained,

> At the beginning, it was frightening to see Indira fall so low, and initially I was just focused on removing all the pressure and giving her the space to feel well again. I also could see that she needed to change jobs for sure, and also something else—like her approach to life or something. So I encouraged her to look for alternatives and figure out what she really wanted to do with her life. Even when she went back to work after her sick leave, I wasn't going to let her off the hook. I worried that she would spiral back down if she didn't figure out a way to change . . . Then gradually, as I watched her wrestle with the question of "What next?" I came to see a silver lining. It was so helpful to see that the struggle was leading somewhere new. I didn't know where that would be, but I could see her transforming in front of my eyes and I thought, "I want some of that for myself."

Witnessing Indira's exploration and reflections made Nick realize that there was more to life than what his aim had been. Before long he was facing the questions of the second transition himself—*Am I who I want to be? What do I really want in my life?* These questions raised Nick's anxiety, which Indira recognized and stepped up to hold:

> Nick had been so important a force when I was questioning everything, I wanted to do the same for him when I saw him starting to fall into his own existential hole. It helped that we'd been through the pattern before, and in many ways, I was still in my journey, still figuring out the "What next?" question. It actually became fun to talk through the possibilities together. That's not to diminish the uncertainty, I mean,

it was really stressful at times, but there was a feeling of being in it together, some kind of complicity in that, a feeling that we would both eventually benefit from this journey.

Indira and Nick spent almost two years in liminality, figuring out what they really wanted. This period was full of highs and lows, false starts and dead-ends, but as we'll see in chapter 7, having each other's support helped them to figure out a new path on which they could both thrive. Moreover, they came to experience their exploration and reflection as benefiting and driving each other forward.

Not all couples whose stories I have collected are like Indira and Nick. On reaching their second transition, some couples instead develop an asymmetric psychological relationship in which the role of the secure base gets permanently lodged with one partner. This means that one partner consistently gives their support to the other, while their partner consistently receives support. Developing this asymmetric secure base relationship is the second trap of the second transition.

Trap 2: Asymmetric Support

Pierre and Camille met in their early forties, when both were working through the breakups of their first marriages. Pierre, a production manager in an automotive manufacturer, had three children and was embroiled in a bitter divorce with his first wife, who had given up her career to support his. Camille, an accountant, had a young daughter and was newly divorced from her first husband, who had tried to pressure her into giving up her career. As Pierre explained, their past experiences made them explicitly agree how to structure their lives, so both could thrive: "I was a pretty bad husband in my first marriage and was determined to change that this time around. I said strongly from the beginning that her career was very important. It was crystal clear for me that it was part of the equation. If I were to be in love with this woman, I should accept her personal expectations in terms of her career."

During their first transition, they decided on a double-primary career prioritization model and set about building a life together that would reflect their choice. Initially, it was plain sailing. Both felt relieved to be free of their previous marriages and reveled in the equality of their relationship. Then, two years into their relationship, Camille hit a professional impasse. She had been, she said, "on autopilot" until the breakup of her first marriage. She had graduated from college, gotten a job as a trainee accountant in a big firm because "that was what smart kids did," and married her childhood sweetheart because, she recalled, "everyone expected me to." While her divorce freed her (a little) from a life of conformity, it saw her reach an impasse on her professional path. She felt trapped in her accounting firm and unhappy being a pair of hired hands. Conscious of his failings in his first marriage, Pierre stepped up to support Camille. He calmly listened to her doubts and questioning, encouraged her to take time to explore alternatives, and pushed her to go for her dreams.

With Pierre as a secure base, Camille decided "to move from the firm to a job as an accounting manager with one of my former clients. It was a big step in terms of gaining autonomy, self-confidence, and really understanding business from the inside." While the move felt right for who she wanted to become as a professional, it was not easy. Camille "moved to an environment that was very male-dominated, an engineering firm. It was a big change, and I struggled in my new role. It was too big a jump, and I really needed Pierre's support."

As the months wore on, Pierre began to feel the weight of constantly being a secure base for Camille. Their double-primary career prioritization meant that he was juggling a demanding career of his own, plus their complex family arrangements. This balancing act made it difficult to provide the constant support Camille needed. At the same time, he was beginning to face his own questions. Like Camille, Pierre had been on what he described as a "train of expectations" since graduating from college. He had become an engineer because that is what smart kids did, and he had joined his company because it was seen as a good employer. He longed to break free, but had no idea where he wanted to go. As Pierre felt the pull to reflect and explore who he wanted to become, he needed Camille to be a secure base for him, but she was so exhausted from her own transition that she could not step up.

"It was a real crisis," explained Pierre, "Camille wanted to make this move, and then she really collapsed. Not because she was not competent but because the job took too much energy. We were both angry at each other. Even though I tried to be available to Camille, it was not enough, and she was angry that I couldn't do more. I was angry with her because I felt I was constantly supporting and got nothing in return, I really needed to make my own transition, but we just couldn't manage the stress."

On her part, Camille realized that she was not supporting Pierre enough but felt that she couldn't give any more. "We thought we had talked a lot about the professional aspect of our lives together, but we realized that this was not the case. Pierre really does support me when he can, but I'm not able to support him, energy-wise. I only understood that very recently. My energy is very focused on my own life, and with our intense family logistics, it is not always easy for me to balance the energy needs."

Must Our Partner Be Our Secure Base?

Pierre and Camille's lives were so packed that they found it hard to have the energy to be a secure base for each other, even though they wanted to be committed to each other's careers and development. Unlike Indira and Nick, who experienced their exploration and reflection as benefiting and driving each other forward, Pierre and Camille experienced Camille's exploration and reflection as holding Pierre's back. This brought them to developmental and relationship deadlocks, which, as we'll see in chapter 7, made it hard for them to find a way out of their second transition.

Like many people, Pierre had a network of support beyond Camille—peers, mentors, and colleagues. So why was the lack of Camille's support so crucial to his individuation journey? I found that most people's relationship with their spouse occupies so much actual and psychological space that filling the gaps of what that relationship does not provide is difficult.[4] This does not mean that your spouse must provide you with everything you need and that there is no room for other relationships, but over time many of us expect this relationship to have a major impact on our life.

While all couples I spoke to struggled to some degree in their second transition, couples with asymmetric support tended to have more conflict than those with mutual support. As Camille and Pierre's story shows, the lack of mutuality builds resentment. Moreover, when couples have asymmetric support, it's harder for both to be able to transition to an individuated path and rebalance the roles they established in their first transition. Such couples can both become stuck on the path they crafted at the end of their first transition, or their paths may diverge, one moving to an individuated path while the other remains stuck—outcomes we'll explore in chapter 7.

You may be wondering whether there are couples in which neither partner is a secure base to the other. While possible, I have not found them. The human desire to support and be supported is a central component of being a couple. Whether this desire gets lodged in one person, as in asymmetric couples, or whether

128

it's passed between partners, as in those with mutual secure base relationships, it's usually present.

I like to think of a mutual secure base relationship as the secret sauce of the second transition. It will give you a way of investing in each other that helps your development, brings you closer together, and makes it much more likely that you both craft new individuated life paths. But is it also helpful at other life stages when you are not in the midst of a big transition? If you are reading this from a different life stage, is it still worth investing in a mutual secure base relationship? The short answer is yes. Why? Because the type of secure base arrangement you have doesn't impact only your transitions but the whole approach you have to your relationship.

Zero-Sum or Positive-Sum Approach?

Broadly speaking, couples have one of two approaches to their relationship—zero- or positive-sum. Couples who see their relationship as *zero-sum* treat their careers, lives, and choices as a pie to be divided between them. The bigger the slice one gets, the smaller the slice left over for the other. I found that most couples with a zero-sum approach had an asymmetric secure base relationship. Like Pierre and Camille, they assumed that they have a finite energy supply and by investing it in one partner, they would deprive the other. This zero-sum mindset pits partner against partner—as one gains, the other loses—and leads to increased relationship tension and conflict.

It's easy to spot a couple with a zero-sum approach because when discussing their relationship, they use the language of trade-offs and compromises. As one woman told me when I asked her why she encouraged her partner's career aspirations while neglecting her own, "Well, you just have to make compromises, don't you, to make all of that work." Every relationship requires compromises. What sets couples with a zero-sum approach apart is that they assume that there is no alternative.

The zero-sum approach is woven into mainstream narratives about dual-career couples. Academics and pundits often portray sustaining two careers as a Herculean task that requires significant trade-offs and compromises from both partners. Contrary to this belief, I found that some couples had a radically different way of seeing their relationship—through a positive-sum approach.

When couples see their relationship as *positive-sum*, they treat their career and personal choices as opportunities to make a bigger pie. They trust that their relationship is strong enough to handle two simultaneously developing lives and careers. I found that most couples with a positive-sum approach had a mutual secure base relationship. Like Indira and Nick, they assumed that one partner's development would have a positive impact on the development of the other, and that one person's gain could benefit the other. All this equates to less relationship tension and conflict.

When couples with a positive-sum approach discuss their relationship, they use the language of mutual benefit. These couples still make compromises, but the need to compromise is not the foundation of their relationship. Instead, their relationship rests on the commitment to find shared fulfillment. And when they do give things up, they see those losses as sacrifices that affirm the value of their relationship. These couples often note how their two career trajectories intertwine and reinforce one another.

What I found most fascinating is that these two approaches have little link to the objective events that happen in couples' lives—they are almost entirely subjective. Imagine two couples in which both partners are simultaneously promoted at work: the first approach their relationship as zero-sum, the second as positive-sum. Partners in the first couple attribute their success to their individual effort and worry that each other's promotion will impinge on their ability to thrive in their own. In response to these concerns, they engage in a tense negotiation in which each tries to get the other to commit to as much practical family support as possible to ensure they have enough time and energy for themselves. While this couple may reach a good practical deal, their tense negotiation erodes goodwill in their relationship. Partners in the second couple, in contrast, attribute their success to their mutual support and celebrate their promotions as a couple success. They know they will need to revisit their practical arrangements, and both most likely will need to make some concessions, but they do it with the objective of finding a mutual solution. In reaching a good practical deal, they have reinforced the mutuality of their relationship and increased the goodwill between them.

Having a mutual secure base relationship, then, doesn't just help you thrive through the second transition; it also fosters a happier relationship over the long term. Given these benefits, it's important that you focus on developing such a relationship, whatever stage of life you are currently in.

Developing a Mutual Secure Base Relationship

I have come across several couples who provide each other with plenty of practical support in their early years—they have figured out a career prioritization that suits them both, and they share parenting and household work—but when the middle years roll in, they do not extend that practical support into the developmental domain by becoming a secure base for each other. As Indira and Nick discovered, being a secure base for your partner can be hard. Yet time after time, I have seen that the couples that survive the second transition and emerge with new life directions are those who have a mutual secure base relationship. There are three things you need to pay attention to in order to foster this type of relationship.

ENCOURAGE EXPLORATION. Genuinely supporting your partner's efforts to explore career alternatives and experiment with different paths is crucial—but it can feel threatening. To minimize the threat, continuous dialogue is vital. Taking an active interest in your partner's impasses, listening to their thoughts, and talking through their dilemmas are all helpful. Most people face setbacks in their explorations, and at these times it's important not to smother your partner with sympathy but to provide a safe harbor and then gently push them back into exploration mode. Although it might feel harsh, you don't do your partner any favors by letting them wallow in their setbacks.

AVOID INTERFERING. There is a fine line between taking an active interest in your partner's exploration and interfering in it. The best support you can give is to lovingly push your partner away from the safety of your relationship and then let them figure out their own path through exploration. Checking whether they have been to that networking event, spoken to that key contact, or read that great book are not helpful things to do. Likewise, resist the temptation to switch from listening mode to advice-giving mode. In times of transition, most people crave a sounding board, not someone who tells them what to do. Finally, although your partner's explorations will make you feel anxious, putting pressure on them to quickly figure out a new path forward will help neither their process nor your relationship. Transitions need time to mature.

PROVIDE EMOTIONAL SUPPORT. Working through an impasse and onto an individuated life path is stressful. Sometimes you will be excited by new possibilities; other times, frustrated by the lack of clarity, disappointed by the options that appear closed, and fearful that you'll never find a way through. Listening to your partner's outpourings and accepting the painful feelings without trying to fix them is the best help you can offer. As we saw in chapter 2, a little undivided attention goes a very long way to building an emotionally supportive relationship.

––––––––––

Having a mutual secure base relationship does not make the second transition easy, but it does give each partner the conditions to do what they must—explore and reflect in liminality to craft an individuated life path. Couples with a mutual secure base relationship pass this psychological role between them. At some points, they are the secure base for the other; at other points, they enjoy that support from their partner. Passing the role back and forth brings mutuality to their relationship and gives them a fuller understanding of what their partner needs and how best to give it.

I know this passing of the secure base role well. Gianpiero and I both push ourselves hard. We regularly leap out of our comfort zones, and we don't always land softly. We can also be excruciatingly hard on ourselves. As a couple, we've developed a turn of phrase that we use when we need the other to be a secure base: "I feel like a blancmange." In my moments of exploration and stretch I worry that—just like the wobbly dessert that my mum served me as a kid in the 1970s—I will collapse onto the plate, reduced to a pile of pink mush. In these moments, I need Gianpiero to stop me from collapsing and at the same time to push me to leap further.

At times it feels that we're constantly swapping the blancmange and the secure base roles between us. And sometimes it's hard to swap, especially to move from being the secure base receiver to the provider. (Try to move blancmange from one plate to another—it's hard and likely messy.) What I've learned in my own couple, and from many others I've spoken to, is that having a mutual secure base relationship doesn't make life easier and more straightforward. Paradoxically, it can make life more challenging. When we have a secure base in our partner, we are more likely to take risks and try new things. It may not make a quiet life, but it certainly makes for an interesting one.

Struggling to Figure Out What We Really Want

Many couples in my research described the struggle period of their second transition as the most difficult one they faced in their entire relationship. Caught by one or both traps, they reached a deadlock from which they could not escape. While much of the work of this struggle period is focused on each partner figuring out what they really want for their future, for couples to successfully pass through the transition, they must find an answer to the question *What do we really want?* I learned that this answer can be found only when couples move beyond their prior career and family agreements and pay attention to their psychological ones. When couples begin developing psychological support, they start to recraft their joint path.

7

Transitioning to a New Path

T o the next adventure!" Wolfgang declared as he clinked mugs of frothing hot chocolate with Heidi. They shared a knowing glance before dissolving into giggles. "If I'd known this weekend would work out so well," she replied, "I'd have suggested it a year ago!"

It was Sunday afternoon, and Heidi and Wolfgang sat in their kitchen, snow lightly falling outside. After eighteen months of debating—often at the top of their lungs—about what they really wanted out of their relationship and their lives, they'd arranged to have two days alone at home with the intention of agreeing a way out of their impasse.

Their married life had been a bit of a roller-coaster ride. The birth of their two children had triggered a period of stress and conflict as they figured out how to manage their new lives as parents with two careers and wrestled their way through their first transition. Nine years of relative stability followed. They had agreed that Wolfgang would have the primary career, and he had risen to a management position at a small manufacturer of digital camera lenses. Heidi had gradually built her expertise as a customer relations specialist while dedicating significant time to their family.

But in their early forties, their hard-earned balance started to unravel. Wolfgang found that he had a gift—and a passion—for mentoring junior colleagues. Encouraged by Heidi, he had enrolled in a part-time coaching course and began to dream of becoming a freelance coach. Every time he considered it, however, he concluded that his family responsibilities made it financially impossible. Feeling increasingly trapped, Wolfgang became resentful and withdrawn at home and his work performance began to suffer.

Meanwhile, Heidi was facing her own impasse. For the past decade, she had deliberately slowed her career progress to focus on the family. Initially, the slower pace felt right, but as her youngest child entered his last year of elementary school, she began feeling regretful. Some of her peers were now on the path to becoming managers while she remained a team supervisor. She was a gifted manager, well respected by colleagues and clients. Wolfgang encouraged her to investigate and apply for a more senior position to pursue her ambition. But how could she take on a management role while keeping up her duties as the chief family organizer? Like Wolfgang, she became resentful of her role in the family and the limits it placed on her career.

Heidi and Wolfgang had always prided themselves on their "no drama" way of life. Now this approach had become stifling. Reluctant to rock the boat, neither of them shared their discontent. Tensions rose; they became snappish and critical with each other and their children.

Things came to a head when Wolfgang's doctor prescribed him a course of antidepressants. Heidi took her surprise as a sign that she had failed to grasp the depth of his suffering. Wolfgang was embarrassed that he hadn't told her more about it before. There was a silver lining, at least. They were now talking again.

They started couples counseling and gradually began to recognize the connection between their impasses. After months of couples work, tensions began to ease and they started to see a way through. Knowing they needed time to figure out the practicalities of change, they'd asked Heidi's parents to look after their kids for the weekend.

Over Saturday and Sunday morning, Wolfgang and Heidi spoke more deeply about their dreams, fears, hopes, and fantasies than they'd ever done before. They were moved and surprised to discover there was more common ground between their future plans than they had imagined. By the time Heidi's parents' car pulled up outside their house, they had agreed that Heidi would accept a promotion she had recently been offered and move into the stable breadwinner position in the family. Her increased salary and their joint commitment to curtail family spending would enable Wolfgang to quit his job, launch a freelance business, and shoulder the role of chief family organizer.

The plan involved some wrenching changes for both of them. Wolfgang would have to relinquish his role as the source of financial stability; he'd have to get used to being economically dependent on Heidi and to stepping up at home. For her part, Heidi would have to accept a secondary role in family life, a shift she found a little frightening. Together, they would have to change their lifestyle, cutting back on family outings and other nonessential expenses until Wolfgang built up his coaching practice.

Would it work? Only time would tell. But at least their path ahead seemed clear.

Laying the Ground for a Broader Path

Like other couples who spoke to me while resolving their second transition, Wolfgang and Heidi were broadening their joint path to accommodate what each of them really wanted out of their careers and lives. Realizing what they wanted to do was an important step, but it was not enough for them to make a successful transition. They needed to lay the psychological ground for their broader path before they cracked the practicalities of embracing it. To do this grounding, they needed to work inside-out.

Successful transitions begin on the inside. They begin with couples renegotiating the roles they play in each other's lives, which in turn shape who they become and what they do. As we explored in chapter 5, couples settle on these roles during their first transition, not always consciously. If couples navigate the first transition well—that is, if their accommodation to their first major live event was deliberate—their roles align with their path. Over time though, these roles constrain couples and need to be renegotiated for them to recraft their path on the basis of their reciprocal individuation.

While Wolfgang and Heidi both had careers and were involved in family life, Wolfgang took the role of the dependable financial provider and Heidi the role of the chief family organizer. In his role, Wolfgang held the ambition, drive, and financial responsibility for the couple, while Heidi held the caring, balance, and family responsibility. Of course, Wolfgang was still caring and Heidi was still ambitious, but neither expressed nor developed these sides of themselves because the other expressed them so well. They thus became polarized and incomplete as individuals but whole as a couple. During their early years, this psychological division of labor worked. As a couple, they were able to progress in their careers, raise a family, and fit into their social world. They also enjoyed an emotionally stable period thanks to their no-drama approach. However, as they hit the struggle of their second transition, these roles and approach became a hindrance.

Their no-drama approach, averse to intense emotional expression, blocked them from sharing their impasses with each other. At the same time, their psychological roles locked them into a life path they no longer wanted. Heidi felt unable to express her growing sense of drive and live out her career ambitions because she was trapped in the role of the chief family organizer. Meanwhile, Wolfgang felt unable to transition to a more balanced career and approach to life because he was trapped in the role of the dependable financial provider. Although they could both see a way forward, neither felt that they could embrace it because they were stuck in complementary roles. To move forward as individuals and as a couple, they would have to betray those familiar roles.

Rebalancing Psychological Roles

Heidi and Wolfgang's experience was common among couples I interviewed for this book. The roles they negotiated in their first transition rarely fit their second. Once couples had wrestled through the struggle of their second transition and identified what they each wanted from their careers, lives, and relationship, they needed to figure out new psychological roles and approaches that fit their broader path.

The first step for Wolfgang and Heidi was to recognize how enmeshed their roles were in their couple, family, and social circles. Although they felt trapped by those roles, those roles also gave them valued identities. Wolfgang was proud of his work progression, which gave him status in his social circle and a unique role at home. His children relied on him for practical advice, and he in turn pushed them to achieve academically. As the son of a breadwinning father, he also felt a sense of comfort and continuity in his position. On her part, Heidi was proud of being the family rock, a role that her mother and most of her female friends also played. Her children's reliance on her made her feel valued and she reveled in helping them develop into interesting and considerate people. She was also proud to juggle a career in parallel to her family life.

Wolfgang and Heidi were ambivalent about changing their roles and having to let go of the clear and cherished identities that those roles afforded them. For months, they wrestled with the fantasy of transitioning to new paths without making any changes to their psychological division of labor. Their fear, one that many couples I spoke to shared, was that to transition, they would need to entirely relinquish the roles they had played to this point and thus lose their valued identities. No wonder they felt trapped.

The reality is that for most couples, Wolfgang and Heidi included, the second transition requires a rebalancing and broadening of roles, not relinquishing them. It is an opportunity for people to undo the polarization of roles in their couple, not reverse it. Each partner needs to reclaim the underdeveloped pieces of themselves that their partner currently holds on their behalf and loosen their grip on, without entirely letting go of, those they hold on their partner's behalf. By embracing new and sharing old roles, couples can move to the psychological center ground. This movement facilitates couples outer-world transitions and make them more multifaceted and psychologically whole. Between embracing new and sharing old roles, most people find the latter the hardest.

The Fear of Rebalancing

Wolfgang feared he would lose the respect of his friends and family if he relied financially on Heidi while he built up his freelancing business. Heidi feared that she would no longer be valued by family and friends if she shared the chief family organizer role with Wolfgang. Both partners' worries concerned their value in the eyes of others. Like most of the couples I spoke to, before their second transition, Wolfgang and Heidi had spent their lives following a life path shaped by social expectations, and their concerns were therefore unsurprising. Looked at through their individuated eyes, neither truly believed their self-worth was attached to their role as financial provider or family rock, yet it was hard for them to escape decades of internalized expectations.

The role of others in Heidi and Wolfgang's transitions was particularly salient because these transitions required them to unpack a traditional gender role divide. This challenge heightened their anxiety about changing, because they rightly assumed that their family and friends would push back against their transition. Every couple I spoke to who made a transition similar to Wolfgang and Heidi's experienced some pushback. Men usually had to deal with offhand comments or jokes; banter between the boys that was used to convey a message. For example, Wolfgang told me that his best friend joked that Heidi would need to give him permission to come out for drinks in the future. Women, on the other hand, usually have to deal with "well-meaning" conversations with friends who are worried about their husband's ability to cope.

Occasionally couples face stronger pushback, usually from extended families. One man I spoke to who, at forty-six, had left his job as a software engineer to pursue his dream of setting up his own business, recounted his father's reaction: "He sat me down and told me it was utterly unacceptable that I had become financially dependent on my wife, and that in doing so I had lost my manhood." Such proclamations are still unfortunately common. Gender norms are changing, but when couples make choices that deviate from traditional norms, it is not unusual for them to encounter hurtful pushback.

It's not just when couples' transitions involve an undoing of gender roles that they experience pushback from others. Remember Carla, whom we met in chapter 5? Her inner-world transition involved stepping back from her constant running approach to life and loosening her grip on the organizer-in-chief role that she played for her family and friends. Yet the more she tried to pull back, the more her family and friends tried to hook her into it. "I couldn't escape," she lamented, "They would tell me I was the best organizer, that they needed me to take charge, that it was my job in the friends' circle. They constantly tried to make me feel guilty. They just could not let me go."

The truth is that whatever psychological role you play, your partner as well as other people in your social circle are often invested in your continuing to play it. Often, they rely on you playing it so they do not have to. If you manage your second transition well, your partner will understand and buy into your need to change. Convincing your friends and wider family can be more challenging.

While on the surface the pushback from others may not seem like a big deal, when you are in the midst of a transition, it hurts. You may feel raw from liminality, a little uncertain, and crave support. You may also have some ambivalence about letting go of your old role, so anything that reaffirms the old can make embracing the new more difficult. Taken together, people's ambivalence toward change and the pushback they experience can slow down or even hinder their transitions.

Rocky First Steps

Alone in their home, Wolfgang and Heidi felt sure that the broader path they had chosen was rooted in their unique interests and desires. They recognized the challenges it posed but were 100 percent behind each other. When they began to transition, however, they discovered that it was harder to make inner changes than outer ones.

Heidi was full of excitement when she accepted her promotion. She gladly worked longer hours and invested the energy required to succeed and progress. What she found hard was to loosen her grip on her role as the family rock. The couple had agreed that Heidi would start work early each day and Wolfgang would pick up the morning madness of breakfast, packing lunches, and doing the school run that used to be Heidi's domain. In spite of this explicit agreement, Heidi constantly worried that Wolfgang would drop the ball on their well-organized family life. She found it hard to accept when he made choices that deviated from hers, and she regularly interfered. Her worries were heightened by her girlfriends and mother, who questioned how well Wolfgang was coping with the demands of the family.

On his part, Wolfgang felt enormous relief when he resigned from his job. He thoroughly enjoyed launching his coaching practice, but the two years it took to build up his business were tough. He found it hard to accept that Heidi outearned him and was embarrassed by his friends' jibes that he was no longer the primary breadwinner. He also felt guilty that his transition had forced the family to rein in their spending and robbed their children of their annual holiday. Wolfgang enjoyed being more actively involved in his kids' lives and balancing this involvement with his career, but he found Heidi's constant interference annoying and resented her helicoptering.

Luckily Wolfgang and Heidi had learned the importance of ongoing dialogue through the difficulties they encountered in the struggle of their second transition. Although the first six months of the new order were rough, they kept talking things through, challenging each other when they found it hard to loosen their grip on their old roles, and encouraging each other to stick with the new path. The thing they spent the longest time working through was their rebalancing of psychological roles. They knew that neither could change without the other. This knowledge helped them to hold each other to account and to work together to deal with the pushback.

Dealing with the Impact on Others

Wolfgang tackled his friends head-on by talking about his love of his new work. They gradually backed off. Some even acknowledged the courage it took him to change and revealed that they wished they could do the same. On her part, Heidi learned to challenge the pushback she received from her mother and friends. She openly praised Wolfgang's role in the family and was honest about her struggles to walk away from the "helicopter wife" position. Her candor was met with respect, and the concerned conversations slowly declined. What surprised them both was how easily their children embraced their transition. Like many couples I have spoken to, they experienced few complaints and minimal pushback from their son and daughter.

Many parents I spoke to imagined that what their children craved above all else was stability. This belief made them wary of making radical changes. Research, however, shows that children themselves like something quite different, especially if it is not caused by an exogenous shock, but proactively initiated within the family. When asked in a study what they would change about the way their parents' work affected their lives, children's most common response was that they wished their parents were less stressed.[1] They weren't concerned about which parent did what, or how many hours they worked. They were concerned with their parents' stress and its impact on them.

Transitioning to an individuated life path will inevitably involve change for a couple's children and likely some stress at the beginning. Over the long term, however, the couple's increased fulfillment is likely to decrease their stress and make their kids happier, accepting of changes in their family life, and less sensitive to social demands.

Wolfgang and Heidi are a couple who navigated the second transition well. They endured a long and hard period of struggle but were able to build a mutual secure base relationship and support each other to find new individuated paths. They faced pushback from friends and family but could shift their roles to the center and lay the ground for a good transition. Two years later, they had stabilized their broader path, and felt content and fulfilled traveling along it. Not all couples follow this pattern. For some, the second transition doesn't lead to reciprocal individuation, but to a frozen path and to a strained or broken relationship.

Developmental Freezing

When people freeze their development, they become stuck on a path that no longer aligns with their interests and desires. While they may still be objectively successful—progressing up a career ladder for example—they feel trapped on a train taking them in the wrong direction. The freezing is developmental because it stops people from becoming the person they desire to be. In this state, people are like caterpillars trapped in their chrysalises, longing to be butterflies but unable to break free.

I found that developmental freezing occurs most often in couples who build an asymmetric secure base relationship during the struggle period of their second transition. Let's return to the story of Camille and Pierre, whom we met in chapter 6, to understand how the freezing occurs. In his previous marriage, Pierre had enjoyed support from his wife but was not given much in return, while Camille's first husband had actively discouraged her career and development. Both wanted a different model for their new relationship, and both were committed to supporting each other in their careers, but their good intentions did not translate into actions. They formed their relationship and entered their second transition hot on the heels of their first. Although they needed each other's support to individuate, after two years together, it became clear that they had an asymmetric relationship in which Pierre was a secure base for Camille, but Camille did not reciprocate this role for Pierre.

What Camille and Pierre had done was to replicate their previous marriages in reverse. Pierre flipped from the "bad husband" to the supportive one who self-sacrificed and got little in return. Camille flipped from the downtrodden wife to the supported one who had no energy to return the support she received. On the surface, the polarization of their roles seemed to benefit Camille and hinder Pierre. With Pierre as her secure base, Camille was able to explore alternative options, reflect on what she wanted, and transition from being a project manager in an accountancy firm to an in-house accounting manager for one of her former clients. Without Camille as his secure base, Pierre could not engage in the exploration necessary to figure out his individuated life path. After two years struggling, he resigned himself to developmental freezing.

When we take a deeper look at Camille and Pierre's situation, we see that the polarization of their roles actually hindered both. As their paths diverged—Camille's becoming increasingly individuated, and Pierre's increasingly frozen—they began to resent each other, and their relationship deteriorated. Their troubles made it hard for Camille to thrive, and it bred resentment in Pierre.

Six months into her new path, Camille shocked her new colleagues by resigning and moving back to her old accountancy firm. "It released a wave of pressure from our relationship," she explained, "We were back on a level playing ground. And it was OK professionally—I mean, it's not like I hated being in the firm." In making this move, Camille sacrificed her individuated life path for her relationship with Pierre. On the surface, they had a relationship that worked practically—they juggled two careers and their complex family life—but they were developmentally stuck. Camille may not have hated her firm, but it kept her stuck in a support role longing to break free. As Pierre described their arrested development, "I feel like we're treading water." They had maintained their relationship but failed to answer the defining question of the second transition—*What do we really want?*—and instead resigned themselves to a frozen path that they followed until hitting their third and final transition.

Not all couples who find themselves in Camille and Pierre's situation resign themselves to a frozen path. Some break up. One woman I spoke to, who divorced in her mid-forties, described her relationship's unraveling as follows, "We were the classic high-flying couple, good jobs, wonderful friends, and we were on a great track. Then in our early forties, we both had crises of confidence. Neither of us felt in the right place. We wanted change, but we didn't know what to move to. We were stuck. I tried to support him, but he didn't really try or couldn't support me. Eventually we retreated to our own worlds. Resentment built, and that was the beginning of the end." Following their divorce, both she and her ex-husband moved to new individuated life paths. While Pierre and Camille sacrificed their individuation for their relationship, this couple chose the opposite. Reflecting on it, the woman recalled, "Looking back, it was as if we needed to break up to be able to move on in our lives."

I found that developmental freezing was relatively common for couples in their second transition, but hardly inevitable. By building a mutual secure base relationship, you can avoid getting stuck and ensure that you both move forward to a broader path.

Cracking the Practicalities of a Broader Path

Once you have figured out what you really want and laid the ground for your reciprocally individuated path, you must switch to managing the practicalities. The more radical the transition you are planning, the more important these practicalities are.

After two years in shared liminality, Indira and Nick, whom we met in chapter 6, gradually settled on what they wanted. They realized that they needed to share the sense of progress and the sense of purpose that had until that point been polarized in their couple. Indira had drifted into her job in corporate communications and had progressed through the ranks to manage the communications team of a midsized logistics firm. The continued sense of progress had kept her motivated through her thirties, but when she hit her forties, she wondered what it was all for.

Although Indira had never been attracted to Nick's career as a teacher, she found herself envying his sense of purpose. He had been drawn to teaching because he wanted to change young people's lives and because he loved math. He acknowledged that he had made a difference in the lives of countless young people, but he felt stuck. "I was living in a perpetual Groundhog Day. Every year repeated itself. Yes, the students changed, but I became overwhelmed with the sameness of it all."

Indira and Nick realized they had been living on opposite ends of a purpose versus progress polarization and both wanted to move to the middle ground. Nick wanted to stay in the world of education but realized that he needed to get out of teaching and into a career that would give him a greater sense of advancement. Indira knew she had to leave the corporate space and seek progress in a realm that was more personally meaningful. Living close to Boston, home to many nonprofit organizations, inspired them to seek new careers in this world. Practically restructuring their lives to make it happen, though, required careful planning.

They had, until that point, relied on Nick's working schedule and holidays to raise their three children and juggle their jobs. With no extended family to turn to during the long summer holidays or for everyday emergencies, how could they manage two middle schoolers and a newly minted high school student? Although comfortably well-off, neither Nick nor Indira earned big salaries, so they could not buy their way out of family logistics problems. With all this in mind, they entered an intense planning phase.

"I felt like we were back in our early thirties, figuring out how we could fit our careers together," recalled Indira, "only this time it wasn't out of a sense of panic but a sense of purpose." Before they applied for new jobs, Indira and Nick mapped out the shape of their future careers. They realized that they would have to invest significant time and energy during their first year in a new job to learn the ropes and get themselves established. Although the couple felt that they had a double-primary career-prioritization model, Nick was definitely the lead parent. During the long school holidays, he took care of almost 100 percent of family logistics, housework, and child care; and during term time, he still managed the lion's share. That would have to change.

Over a series of weeks, they developed what Nick referred to as their "new pact." They first agreed to stagger their transitions: Indira trying to make the move to a nonprofit first to establish herself, and then be ready to pick up more at home when Nick made his transition. On the home front, they agreed to move to a true co-parenting model and engage their teenage children to help out more. Neither thought these changes would be easy, but both realized they could not successfully transition without making them. Finally, they agreed that they would revisit their pact every six months to ensure they were on target and keeping each other to their promises.

Indira and Nick's story illustrates how couples need to revisit agreements forged in their first transition to successfully complete their second. First, it's helpful to map the projected shapes of your transitions, and subsequent career paths will reveal the relative levels of investment, and peaks and troughs of pressure, that you will need to balance. The career-mapping exercise I explained in chapter 4 will help you here. Armed with this realistic picture, you will then need to revisit, and potentially renegotiate, your career-prioritization and parenting agreements. Again, you might want to refer back to chapter 4 for a guide on how to do this. Lastly, just as Indira and Nick negotiated their "new pact," the cusp of a transition is the perfect time to redo the couple contracting exercise outlined in chapter 2. This will help orient and ground you in the coming years.

Struggling to Make It Work

Some couples agree on what they both want, lay the psychological ground, but simply cannot agree on or make the practicalities work.

We Just Can't Afford It

Having mapped out their transitions, some couples I spoke to reached the disheartening conclusion that they simply could not afford to make changes they would have liked. Launching into a period where one partner has little or no income while they retrain or build a new business feels unaffordable. Likewise, some couples were so financially committed to a mortgage or heavy costs of living that the prospect of one partner moving to a job with a permanently lower salary felt impossible.

Khalil and Amal found themselves in this situation when Amal decided that her individuated path would be to set up her own business. Until that point, she had worked in an events-organizing company and had provided the couple with stability, both financial and emotional. In contrast, Khalil had set up a small business and had lived out the couple's excitement and risk-taking. As a couple, they were optimistic and lived to the fullest, but they were not financially prudent. They had a hefty mortgage and few savings.

Khalil understood Amal's frustration with the corporate world and realized it was time to share some of the excitement of entrepreneurship with her. He was prepared to shoulder his share of the family stabilizer role. But neither he nor Amal could figure out how to afford Amal's transition. She had developed a solid business plan with a friend to launch an events company specializing in corporate retreats. Both she and her friend had experience in this area and felt they could steadily build up a solid income stream—steadily, but not quickly enough to cover her and Khalil's financial commitments. After months of back-and-forth, the couple concluded that Amal needed to shelve her plans. They committed to tightening their belts and start saving, but both knew it would take several years to build a nest egg big enough to enable the transition.

Khalil and Amal's story is discouraging, but hardly unique. Its not unusual for couples to get trapped on a financial treadmill. Many just don't make enough to build significant savings after all their expenses are paid off. Some, even as their salaries grow, stretch themselves to buy a bigger house, locking themselves into a cycle of spending more as they earn more. It's natural to reward yourself for your success, but rewarding only through spending locks you into always needing the income level you currently enjoy or more. If you think long-term, saving is a much better reward because it buys you the option to change in the future.[2] One of the key benefits of being in a dual-career couple is that two incomes can provide a financial cushion to enable transitions, but realizing this benefit takes self-control, planning, and of course an element of luck.

We Just Cannot Agree

What happens if you understand each other's desire to transition and support changes to your psychological roles and agreements, but simply cannot agree with each other's new career plans? Margot and Jeff found themselves in this dilemma at the end of their second transition. When they met in their mid-thirties, neither anticipated major hurdles in juggling their careers and relationship. Both were committed to their work and to each other, neither wanted children, and they were like-minded on most aspects of life. What could go wrong?

Fast-forward to their mid-forties, and they entered the familiar pattern of restlessness with what they had and questioning what they really wanted. Both agreed that they wanted more adventure and excitement in their lives and careers, and they wanted to break free from the constraints they had accepted in exchange for stability and progress until that point. Everything seemed to align, except that they had very different ideas of what adventure and excitement looked like.

Margot longed to live abroad. She had backpacked around Southeast Asia as a college student and thought it would be fun to live the expat life in that region. They could explore new countries and experience a totally different life. She didn't anticipate a permanent move but was set on a three- to five-year period. They had no kids, their parents were young, and they could easily rent out their apartment and cover the mortgage. Why not take the plunge?

Jeff, however, wanted to plunge into very different waters. In the previous five years, he had developed an expertise in a sought-after aspect of forecasting technology and he longed to set himself up as a freelance adviser in this area. It would be low risk. Several companies had already asked him to consult for them, he had a large network, and with a little luck he stood to earn more than his current salary. The issue was that he firmly believed he needed to remain in the United Kingdom to make this career move.

For months, Margot and Jeff tried to sell each other their preferred options. Margot argued that Jeff would be able to set up his freelancing from any location in the world, while Jeff argued that Margot could find adventure through a career move rather than a geographical move. Neither budged, and they reached a stalemate.

What can you do if you find yourself in Margot and Jeff's situation, when your ideal paths conflict such that pursuing one makes the other impossible? First, it's helpful to know that these situations are not necessarily deal breakers. Deal breakers typically arise when one of you wants to have children and the other doesn't, when one of you wants to permanently live in a country that the other could not tolerate, or when you want to live according to very divergent values. In these situations, you may be better off in a relationship with someone else. For everything else, you can usually find a compromise with an investment of time and effort.

Seeking professional mediation when in stalemate is particularly helpful. Your friends and family will all have their own opinions and ideas on what you should do. But what you need is someone to impartially help you explore the dilemma—to see it through different eyes without telling you what to do. This is the route that Margot and Jeff took.

Although their relationship was still strong, they entered marriage counseling with the explicit aim of working through their deadlock. Over the course of a few months, they recognized how important each other's transitions were and looked for ways in which both could get what they wanted. They decided that Margot would take a year's secondment to her company's Hong Kong office while Jeff stayed in London to strike out as a freelance consultant. They could manage a long-distance relationship for that period, and the flexibility of Jeff's new freelancer life meant that he could visit several times during the twelve months.

Jeff resigned six weeks before Margot boarded the plane for Hong Kong. Over that year, they both thrived in their adventures and enjoyed professional success. Jeff warmed to the idea of moving abroad, but when the year ended, Margot returned to the UK. They agreed that the next two years would be spent in London while Jeff established his freelance business, and then they would return to Asia together for a second stint. Not the ideal solution for either, but one that was good enough for both.

Embracing What We Really Want

Figuring out what you really want and transitioning to a broader individuated path together will not resolve all your questions. Nor should it. The questions we face in our second transition—*Where does my passion lie? Am I who I want to be? What should I do with the rest of my life?*—are long-term developmental projects. The best we can do is partially answer them and then continue to live them. As Rainer Maria Rilke, the Austrian poet and novelist, wrote in his *Letters to a Young Poet,*

> . . . have patience with everything unresolved in your heart
> and to try to love the questions themselves as if they were

locked rooms or books written in a very foreign language. Don't search for the answers, which could not be given to you now, because you would not be able to live them. And the point is, to live everything. Live the questions now. Perhaps then someday far in the future, you will gradually, without even noticing it, live your way into the answer.[3]

If you can embrace your new individuated life while continuing to live your questions, you will enjoy a stable period of shared growth before your third transition begins. Then, with some luck, you may find that you have lived your way into the answers.

What Do We Really Want?

NATURE OF THE TRANSITION

Shift focus from adapting to social demands and expectations to identifying and pursuing what each partner wants out of their careers, lives, and relationship.

TRIGGERS

A combination of two forces—the drive to individuate that is part of the life cycle and the need to tackle the division of roles within a couple that is a consequence of the first transition.

DEFINING QUESTION

What do we really want?

Each partner must identify their unique interests and desires and the couple must figure out how they can help each other pursue them.

TRAPS

Mistrusting our partner's explorations and becoming defensive

Not mutually supporting each other's development

RESOLUTION

Mutual individuation

Building a mutual secure base relationship that allows both partners to individuate

Rebalancing roles each partner plays in the other's life

Renegotiating the division of career and family labor that they established in their first transition

TOOLS

Develop a mutual secure base relationship: Understand how best to support your partner in their transition and build mutuality in your relationship (chapter 6)

REFLECTIONS

Relational resilience: Tips on how to build a high-quality connection with your partner that can withstand adversity (chapter 5)

TRANSITION
THREE

Who Are
We Now?

8

Loss and Limits

Noam lay quietly in bed, gazing thoughtfully at Shira's sleeping form. Decades of experience had altered the fierce beauty of her youth. Her curves had softened, her long, straight hair was now more silver than brown, and sun spots mottled her strong hands.

Noam's body, once lithe and muscular like the long-distance runner he had been, had also been changed by time. The bulge around his waist, the persistent dull aches in his joints, and the eyeglasses he now relied on were constant reminders that he was well into middle age. Still rattled by the sudden death of a childhood friend six months ago, Noam was keenly aware of his own mortality. If Itai, a paragon of healthy living, could be taken by a heart attack without warning, when would Noam's time be up?

As it had happened often lately, an overwhelming sense of loss swept over him. It wasn't the loss of youth or even the potential approaching of death that saddened him—it was the loss of possibility. He had once dreamed of being a senior manager in a big advertising firm, a dream that he now knew would never be realized. Their son would shortly be leaving home for college. Noam would miss cheering on his basketball team.

But most difficult to face was the sense of loss in his relation-ship with Shira. Their once-passionate bond was now mainly platonic. The love was still there, but its texture had changed. Since they had moved six months earlier, Noam felt as though he scarcely knew his wife of twenty-five years. And he wondered if she was still interested in him.

Noam and Shira had had their fair share of ups and downs over their first two transitions, but never a major crisis. The in-fertility that plagued their early thirties had been heartbreaking and put their life on hold for five years until Daniel, their "miracle baby," had arrived. Although both had dreamed of international careers, they agreed to stay in Israel so that Daniel could enjoy their tight-knit extended family and its large band of cousins. They had several happy years cocooned in their families, and built a bank of joyful memories of holidays, relaxed weekends, and special times. When their forties rolled in, Noam and Shira wrestled with questions of direction. Both eventually decided to delay big professional transitions until Daniel left home, which was about to happen.

As his eyes wandered around their darkened bedroom, Noam noticed a cardboard box filled with family photos, still unpacked from the move. It struck him as an apt symbol of their marriage— forgotten in a corner while their lives went on. Were they facing a new life, or staring at old age? He was not sure. Who was Shira now? Who was he? And perhaps most frightening, who were they?

This moment of uncertainty hadn't come as a surprise to Noam and Shira. They'd seen friends face a crisis of identity in their fifties, and they were determined to avoid the marital woes many of those friends had suffered. Their solution: "To start a big adventure before Daniel leaves home," as Shira put it.

They had often dreamed of living in Europe and were partic-ularly drawn to the Netherlands and France, where they also had family. Daniel's desire to attend college outside Israel had only strengthened their resolve to move. They figured the move would give Daniel a platform to get into a good college, and once he left home, they would be perfectly placed to explore a new country and cultivate new shared interests.

The big adventure came to fruition through a career opportunity for Shira—a new job with an R&D team in Amsterdam. The job offer was a ticket to a new life in Europe for the family. Noam's career was on a plateau, and realizing he would not progress further, he was half-content, half-resigned to become a freelancer, capitalize on his experience, and focus on making their move a success. The family left their longtime home in Tel Aviv and started life anew.

But somehow, the feeling of being stuck that they'd hoped to avoid caught up with them despite the move. They worried that Daniel was the glue that kept them together, and that when he left home next year, they would fall apart. For the past twenty years, they realized, they'd been caught in a frantic cycle of doing. Now they discovered they'd lost the sense of what being together meant—what it felt like, even. They also realized that the focused life they had been living—career and family—was not enough. As they reached the later stage of their careers, their thoughts broadened. What had been their impact on others? Would they leave a legacy? Had they made a difference in the world?

Noam sighed. "Now I understand the meaning of the old saying, 'You can run, but you can't hide.'" He shifted his weight in bed and stared at the ceiling, resigned to another restless night.

The Third Transition Begins

The final transition comes at a time of dramatic shifts in roles. As we enter this stage of our careers, spanning our fifties to retirement, the stability of the path we crafted at the end of our second transition is challenged by these role shifts, the identity voids they open up, and the legacy questions they raise that go to the core of our being in the world.

These role shifts are inextricably linked to our career and life stage. Our careers plateau; our bodies are no longer what they once were; our kids, if we had any, leave home. Having raced through decades of career growth and child rearing, we wake up alone with a person who might seem to have changed dramatically from the one with whom we originally fell in love. We are that person, too. The empty space around us and the void that lurks into the no longer unimaginable future make us face fundamental questions of identity: *Who am I now? Who do I want to be for the rest of my life?*

Confronting these questions makes us face the fact that we have reached some limits. We become acutely aware of how the paths we crafted and the relationship patterns we established in our first two transitions shaped where we are now and the options that are available to us in the future.

Career Limits

As couples enter the third transition, they face what Shira described as "a wave of loss and vulnerability." I found that at this time, most couples lose the illusion that, with their partner's support, they can be in control of their destinies. People's shifting roles make their lives feel more precarious. And these feelings hit them from all sides at once.

Hardest to deny are the physical limits people run into at this life stage. Stamina drops, as does the ability to burn the candle at both ends. People face health issues, be they niggling aches and pains or more serious medical conditions. Like Noam, most people inevitably experience the death of friends, parents, and other loved ones. There is no denying that half your life has passed, which makes you wonder how long your health will last, and when your time will be up. If you hadn't before, you can't avoid questioning the assumption that everything is possible.

Professionally, many of the people I spoke to came to a plateau in the final stages of their careers. They had reached, or were close to reaching, the most senior roles they could, and as they looked around their organization, they saw that the majority of their colleagues now belonged to younger generations. No longer the rising stars, they were now managing those—if they were lucky. Others' potential outstripped their own and, at best, the bright young things turned to them for support and wisdom. Some people even wondered if the bright young things were impatiently waiting to take their place.

For some people, these changes come as an unexpected shock. One man I interviewed was fifty-three when he learned that he was up against one of his forty-four-year-old subordinates for a promotion to sales director. Having believed that this subordinate was his protégé, he suddenly faced the reality that he was his competitor. "It was a huge blow when I found out," he told me. "Not only had my protégé not told me that he was applying for the role, I realized that most people around us assumed that he would get it. The thought of being leapfrogged by a guy ten years my junior was really hard to bear. It was an enormous wake-up call."

This man had always thought of himself as a high-potential, but when he talked to colleagues, he realized that he was now seen as one of the "old guard"—a stable, benign force that kept the ship sailing straight, but that didn't create big waves. He certainly didn't feel "old" and did little "guarding," and he hated the idea of becoming one of the organization's "dinosaurs," as he put it. But if he wasn't willing to be one of the old guard and wasn't seen as a high-potential, who was he now as a professional? And given that he had at least fifteen years left in his career, who did he want to become?

The questions that this man faced suddenly because of a job opening, others encounter more gradually. As our careers plateau, we feel our ambitions shifting. They ask, *Is this it? I have invested so much in my career, now what?* Many people are not yet ready to throw in the towel, but neither do they want to go on as before. This is a time to take stock and reassess.

Parenting Losses

Alongside changes to professional identities, couples I spoke to at this stage who had children also needed to contend with changes to their identities as parents. As their children left home for college and took their first steps on their journey into adulthood, they became less active participants in their daily lives. This shift made many, particularly those who had taken the lead parent role, feel superfluous: *Who am I now if I am not a hands-on parent? What should I do now that I am no longer needed so much?*

For twenty-three years, Zara had taken the lead parent and the secondary career role, following Mohammed while he pursued his global career working in a mining company. Zara had enjoyed raising their three children and had always worked along the way. The year their youngest child left for college, however, Zara hit a wall: "I lost such a big part of my life, a part of my identity. I was the center of the family, and then suddenly it was just Mohammed and me. I wondered if I was still useful, still valuable." Like some other lead parents I spoke to, Zara's self-worth and self-esteem tumbled when her children left home. Describing her greatest fear, she candidly admitted that she dreaded "becoming a bitter old woman who watches her children flourish and complains about being left behind."

Seeing your children flourishing in the world of possibilities that you once faced can fill you with pride and loss in equal measure. You want the best for them, of course, and yet you're reminded that the future no longer lives with you, in more than one way. Noam, for example, recounted how his son Daniel's summer backpacking trip around European cities had made him "ache with the memories that it used to be me." Our children's adventures in the world are constant reminders of a youth that is now gone.

Inevitably, changing identities as parents make people face their changing relationship as a couple. Parenting is a project that binds many couples together. It is the project for whose sake we sweep our differences under the carpet and keep up the pretense that all is okay. When children leave home, the necessity to simply keep going leaves with them.

The losses that come from these shifts in roles and the identity voids that they open up are real, and the questions they raise pressing. But the shifts also reveal a glimmer of new possibilities.

Emerging Opportunities

The period after children leave home used to signal the twilight years of a career, followed by retirement, grandparenting duties, and steadily declining health. This is no longer the case. For starters, our life expectancy is increasing, as are the number of years we can expect to be healthy.[1] If you were born in the West in the 1960s, you have a more than 50 percent chance of living to at least ninety-two; if you're a child of the 1970s, you have a 50 percent chance of living to at least ninety-five; fast-forward to the 1980s and if you're in the lucky top 50 percent, you should reach at least ninety-eight.[2]

As our life expectancy rises, so does the delay between children leaving home and becoming parents themselves.[3] Taken together, this can equate to two decades or more of reasonable health when we are free from intensive parenting and grandparenting responsibilities and are able to work and deal with whatever life offers us.

This new period, which few previous generations enjoyed, opens up a range of emerging opportunities that dual-career couples are often well-placed to grasp. Because they have enjoyed earning two salaries for most of their working lives, they are likely to have a larger financial buffer than couples with just one breadwinner. Likewise, life's big expenses are behind them—a mortgage may already be paid off, and college fees are the last lump before the kids' expenses decline. All this means they have a little more financial freedom than they might have enjoyed before— financial freedom that can give them a platform to make changes in their lives.

Alongside these financial changes, many couples enjoy a renewed level of flexibility. With kids gone from the home, they are no longer tied to a set location; they can travel outside of school holidays or even consider uprooting and moving somewhere new. While few couples are wealthy enough to retire early, they may have more options in this stage than we have previously enjoyed. Freelancing, a portfolio career of part-time roles, and entrepreneurship (all of which we'll explore in chapter 9) are potential options for those couples who want to make career changes. And with twenty years of working life left, more and more over-fifties are retraining and making radical career transitions.

The emergence of these opportunities coincides with a change to our ambitions. People may not now strive for a singular goal— to reach the top of our profession or to become an expert in our chosen field. Instead, I found that they often have ambitions in multiple domains that they strive to balance. Professional success may still be important, but so is the pursuit of new interests, the rekindling of old, and time to dedicate to family and friends. Thoughts of legacy and meaning are also common in this transition. Because we are anxious not to waste time, the tension between these emerging opportunities and our feelings of loss creates a sense of urgency. Urgency to use time well. Urgency to live life to the fullest. And urgency to figure out who we are now and who we want to become.

I Must Figure This Out

If our twenties and thirties are the "should" decades where we feel compelled to establish our careers and families, and our forties are the "want" decade where we craft our individuated life path, then our fifties and beyond are the "must" decades. The sense of urgency people feel is palpable. As Noam and Shira's story illustrates, this urgency can quickly translate into decisive action. If you are going to do things differently and become different people, it must happen now. Now is the time to reassess. Now is the time to consider your legacy. Now is the time to make things happen—or they just won't.

One advantage of facing this urgency in our third transition is that it comes at an age when we have learned to be kinder to and easier on ourselves. When we say *I must*, we are no longer striving for perfection, we are striving for good enough. And research shows that good enough is the best route to contentment for us and those around us.

When people aim for good enough, as opposed to perfection, they are on average more satisfied with their lives, happier in their careers, optimistic about the future, and content with the choices they make.[4] People are also better parents when they let go of ideals and strive instead to be good enough.[5] As Gail Sheehy remarks in her book on life transitions, "Would that there were an award for people who come to understand the concept of enough.

Good enough. Successful enough. Thin enough. Rich enough. Socially responsible enough. When you have self-respect, you have enough; and when you have enough, you have self-respect."[6] Having a "good enough" approach is better in almost all our life domains. Except, it turns out, in our relationship.

When Good Enough Is Not Enough

In his book *The All or Nothing Marriage*, Eli Finkle charts the history of the Western world's approach to marriage from the days when it was scarcely more than an economic transaction to the recent emergence of what he terms the *self-fulfilling marriage*. Finkle reveals a simple but important trend: that we are expecting more and more from our relationships.[7] Good enough is no longer enough.

For a long time, people associated a good relationship with love, support, and lots of sex. It was also anticipated that as time passed, the passion in relationships would be replaced by companionship. The first thing that changed was the societal expectation that love, support, and physical passion should persist, not evolve, as relationships age. Nowadays, when the sex and passion drain from relationships like Noam and Shira's, alarm bells ring and deeper relational problems emerge.

The second thing to change was that over the past thirty years, we have added another layer to these expectations—a layer of self-development. Western society now portrays, and most people in the West now see, a good relationship as one in which each partner knows the other well and encourages them to become their best selves and to reach their full potential. Researchers have called this role we expect our partners to play the *Michelangelo phenomenon*, in recognition of the artist's approach to sculpture.[8] The great master famously explained that he never created a sculpture; instead, he chipped away at the marble until he released the figure that had always lain sleeping within. In his own eyes, Michelangelo was not the creator of his famous statues, he was their liberator. In a similar way, we don't yearn for our partner to mold us, but for them to help us grow toward and release our best and authentic self. We want them to be committed not only to us, but also to our development and to our potential. This was exactly what people I interviewed craved from their partner during their second transition.

One of the most well-known models of human psychology, Maslow's hierarchy of needs, depicts a pyramid with our most basic needs for food, warmth, and safety at the foundation and our need for reaching our full potential—what Maslow termed *self-actualization*—at the very top. According to his theory, we only turn our attention to needs at the top of the pyramid when those at the bottom of the pyramid have already been met.[9] Following this logic, couples should see the new layer of self-development as the icing on their relationship cake, as something to strive for when everything else is going smoothly. But here's the rub: couples don't see self-development as the cake's icing, they see it as one of the cake's ingredients. Even if every other dimension of our relationship is good enough, if our partner is not interested in helping us reach our full potential, then we feel the relationship is not enough.

The Rise of Gray Divorce

This lack of care for each other's development is what led Eleanor and Christoph, whose story I introduced in chapter 3, to the edge of breakup in their mid-fifties. If you recall, Christoph talked about their multi-decade quest of having it all and doing it all that in their early years had felt meaningful, but in hindsight had resulted in them neglecting their relationship and each other's growth.

Both medical doctors, Eleanor and Christoph had always had high ambitions. They had poured enormous investment into their careers and into raising two children. They had both progressed to senior roles in their hospitals, taken on extra volunteer work, spent time with their children, and maintained the lifestyle they wanted. From home-cooked food to regularly entertaining friends, and from closely monitoring kids' homework to volunteering on their school's parents association, Eleanor and Christoph did it all. All, that is, except invest in each other. Eleanor summed up the state of their relationship in their early fifties as follows: "On the surface, we have everything—everything we have ever wanted—but it's not enough. In the process of getting all this stuff, our relationship has become empty and a gulf has grown between us."

While making sure that everything was going well on the surface, Eleanor and Christoph had stopped taking an active interest in the highs and lows of each other's lives and stopped pushing each other to become their best selves. They had also stopped paying attention to what Christoph referred to as "the small stuff." They put petty disagreements to the back of their minds rather than working them through together. They held on to small disappointments rather than airing them. Over the years, this accumulation of small stuff resulted in a gulf filled with resentments and blame.

In the day-to-day hustle and bustle of their thirties and forties, putting aside the small stuff made sense. There was always something urgent to deal with for the kids or to just simply keep their family machine running. Only when they looked back did they realize the damage they had done turning their relationship, too, into a machine of sorts. Both felt uncared for and lonely, and wondered how—and indeed whether—they could bridge the gulf they had created. Christoph lamented, "I don't think she's interested in my life anymore, in who I can be. And I don't know how, or even if, we can rekindle that."

Eleanor and Christoph's story reveals a common pattern. As life gets busy in the early and middle years, many couples stop investing in each other and in their relationship. These couples often have a solid bond, they are stable, they love each other, and they may have a strong physical connection. But they have given up trying to sculpt each other into their best selves and given up being curious about each other's developmental journey. They have also let the little things build up. Day to day, it's easy to ignore these little things, and many of us tell ourselves we should, but eventually they amount to a huge can of worms that is daunting to open. Eleanor and Christoph's story also illustrates how decisions we make and patterns we embed in our early years can lead us to impasses in later life. Their well-intentioned quest to have it all eroded their relationship to the point where both doubted it could be saved.

While we might want a relationship that fosters our self-development and a partner who knows our whole selves, cultivating this kind of relationship takes long-term investment. It takes constantly paying attention to the little things about our relationship, and at the same time keeping an eye on the future and how our partner wants to grow. When this investment ceases, our couple may survive but not thrive.

As life changes pace in the later stages of our career, many of the couples I studied at this stage became painfully aware that surviving is not good enough. They wanted more, they had time to make a change, and with their sense of urgency they were compelled to do something about it. As we'll see in chapter 9, for some couples, this means opening that can of worms and reinvesting in each other to kick-start their relationship and together figure out who they are and who they want to become. For others, it means going their separate ways.

The rise of so-called gray divorces has been well documented. In the United States alone, the divorce rate has doubled in the over-fifties since the 1990s.[10] Why? It comes back to the tension between the sense of loss and the glimmer of new opportunities we explored earlier. People who are unsatisfied with their good-enough relationships face the prospect of plenty of healthy productive years ahead, they have more financial freedom than ever in the past, and want more for themselves.[11] All this makes taking the plunge into a new relationship more appealing and less risky than in years gone by. And increasingly it is women, with their newfound financial freedom, rather than men who are initiating these divorces.[12] The rise of gray divorces has led to another trend, that of late love.

Late Love

In her heartwarming book *Late Love*, Avivah Wittenberg-Cox tells her own story of late love and draws lessons for others who are experiencing or looking for the same.[13] Two patterns she describes were also reflected in the couples I interviewed who had found late love. First, late love presents a paradox of complexity. On the one hand, because it arrives after the usual child-rearing age, and at a time when our careers are well established, couples' first transition is simpler; it usually concerns money and home, not careers and children. On the other hand, partners both bring a complex web of relationships into their new love: children who may resist the breakdown of their previous relationship, friends who might side with their old partner, and aging parents who find it hard to understand their choices. Late love is thus simpler yet more complex than love that blossoms in our early years. Second, couples that form at this life stage are very committed to getting their relationship right and often make painstaking efforts to avoid mistakes of the past.

Olivia found late love after emerging from a painful divorce in her early fifties. A year previously, she had discovered that her husband had been cheating on her, which she described as the straw that broke the camel's back. Their relationship had been long deteriorating, and she had been sticking with it for the sake of their teenage children. But the betrayal was too much to bear. She rented an apartment, loaded her car with her most prized possessions, and made a break for freedom.

Looking back on her first marriage, Olivia understood why it had unraveled. "I didn't see it at the time, but now it's so clear what went wrong. We simply stopped devoting ourselves to each other. Instead we devoted ourselves to work and to the children. Our relationship got lost along the way. Petty resentments gradually built, and we began to blame each other for our failings."

On a trip home to visit her elderly parents, Olivia bumped into Will, a childhood sweetheart whose parents lived on the same street as hers. The pair bonded around their respective divorces and after six months of increasingly frequent meetings, they embraced their late love.

Will's marriage had ended differently, but no less acrimoniously than Olivia's. "It sounds cliché, but we just grew apart. We invested everything in our daughter, and when she left home there was nothing left. What I regret is that toward the end, the relationship got nasty. We would criticize each other, take constant swipes. It was very hurtful. Meeting Olivia was a breath of fresh air after that."

Whether we fall in love at eighteen or eighty, the initial emotional experience is the same. The giddy sense of connection, the way the other person inhabits our thoughts, the feeling of excitement. Will recounted his early days with Olivia, "It was like we were nineteen again. I was happier than I had been in decades." Both Olivia and Will were determined to build a supportive, loving relationship, but their previous ones made them approach it with caution. "We were two prickly hedgehogs," explained Olivia, "both worried that we would spike the other, and worried about being spiked ourselves."

For two years, they kept separate houses as they felt their way into their new love. They also had to manage strong resistance from Olivia's children, who initially refused to meet Will, still hanging onto the hope that Olivia would reconcile with their father. Career-wise, both Olivia and Will were in stable positions, but the changes to their personal lives made them begin to question who they were as professionals. "We had a lot to figure out," Will told me, "If we could become different people personally, could we also become different people in our careers?"

Many late-love relationships begin, like Olivia and Will's, after the breakdown of previous ones. Sometimes they follow the death of a much-loved partner; and occasionally people find their first love later in life. Whatever way these couples form, all partners in late love face the questions of identity that all couples face in this life stage.

Who Are We Now?

Whatever the path that brings a couple to their third transition, and whatever stage their relationship is in—from new love to thirty-plus years of marriage—it is not enough to ask *Who am I now?* Couples must jointly ask *Who are we now?* Answering this question is the developmental task of couples in their third transition. Just like the other transitions, couples that work figure out the answer to this question together. This figuring out is a quest for self-discovery that requires couples to reassess the past and to reimagine the future. Just like the other two transitions, the third contains traps. If you can navigate these successfully, then together you will chart a new path of renewal in your love and work.

In chapter 9, we will explore the traps that can ensnare couples as they wrestle through the struggle period of this final transition. We will focus on the process of self-discovery and the ways in which you can grasp the opportunity that this life stage offers. Then, in chapter 10, I will share the stories of three couples that work. These couples each worked through their identity questions and crafted generative paths out of their third transition.

Before we move into the heart of the third transition, I'll share here a key pattern I saw among couples who had more than good-enough relationships, and in couples who grew through their third transition together.

Shared Passions

Many things in life cannot be predicted or planned, but the role shifts that occur in our fifties can be. Children always (eventually) leave home, our careers always mature, and none of us can escape physical aging. Couples need to readjust to these changes. The third transition can be rocky if the main focus of your couple has been your careers and kids. Time and time again, I saw in my research that the couples who had strong relationships over the long term were those who had shared passions.

A shared passion is something that you engage in together, that concerns neither your careers nor your children. It is an expression of who you are as a couple and is an important way of maintaining a shared sense of "we." The couples I have spoken to have a huge variety of shared passions, from playing in a music band together, to running a scout group, to sailing, to renovating and reselling houses. Some of these passions are big, others small; some ongoing, others sporadic. What they have in common is they provide a space for a couple to come together in service of a joint interest or goal.

For one couple I interviewed, that shared passion was opera singing. They fell in love rehearsing for a production of Mozart's *Don Giovanni* in their local operatic society, and their passion for song and for each other remained strong ever since. As their careers got busy and kids arrived, they no longer had time to perform in full productions, but they didn't drop their passion. "We always sing," exclaimed the husband, "in the kitchen, in the car, when we're happy, when we're sad. It binds us together. We also practice together. We love to perform classic arias. Our friends and family often ask us to perform together at celebrations, birthdays, weddings. We've even occasionally performed at work gatherings." His wife added that they were referred to as "the duet" and that this shared identity is a source of pride for them both.

Having a shared passion does not mean that you do it all the time, nor that it is the only thing you do outside of your careers and children, but it does mean that you have a special space for each other—a space somewhat immune to the smoldering of romance. Many of the couples I spoke to had shared passions in the early years of their relationship, but these often got dropped in the intensive middle years when they were squeezed by the demands of an accelerating career and a demanding family. Building up these shared passions before children leave home is especially valuable.

When their youngest child entered eleventh grade, one woman I interviewed gave her husband Latin dancing lessons for his birthday. The ten-week course was the first new thing they had done together for more than fifteen years, and through it they developed a love for dance and a renewed love for each other. "For the first time in years, we were novices together. We were both learning from scratch, and it gave us the freedom to play and be a bit silly. We laughed so much, more than we had in a long time," her husband recounted. Over the next three years, they added a book club and a walking club to their repertoire. These new-found shared passions certainly helped their relationship: more unexpectedly, they also helped their children. "The kids are enthusiastic about our new activities," the woman told me. "I think it grounds them to see that we are doing something together. And I do think it's the activities that anchor us as a couple and them as kids."

Gianpiero and I have not yet reached our third transition, but the idea of shared passions is one I often reflect on in our relationship. We are a couple who do a lot together. I imagine the phrase "joined at the hip" could apply to us. We share a love for running, the outdoors, skiing, and cooking, and we work together. And I don't just mean that we work at the same place; I mean we actually work together—we research, write, and even occasionally teach together. For all the time we spend together, however, I realize that everything we do revolves around our work or our family. We don't yet share a passion that is just about us, with no work, no kids, involved.

I can easily justify this. Our kids are at an amazing age where they are keen to do everything, and they still want to do it with us. And we're very aware that this will come to an end soon. We also love and are very dedicated to our careers. At the same time, I take the patterns I find in my research seriously. Developing a shared passion that is just ours is on my couple to-do list for the next few years.

9

Exploring Wider Horizons

Norah slumped onto the sofa, her eyes red from a day of tears. Attending her mother's funeral had been one of the most difficult experiences of her life. Jeremy settled down next to her and put an arm around her. It was more than twenty years since his mother had passed away, but he was still in touch with the grief.

"I guess it's us next," said Norah.

Jeremy resisted replying. Now was not the time.

The last two years had brought immense change for Norah and Jeremy. It began when both their fathers had passed away unexpectedly within five weeks of each other. One stroke and one heart attack had left them reeling. They became caregivers of Norah's ailing mother just at the time when their children were flying the nest.

Max, their eldest, had left to attend engineering college. Dylan, their youngest, had won a scholarship to complete his last two years of high school at a residential sports academy. Having become parents at forty, these changes unfolded as Norah and Jeremy entered their late fifties, a time when their careers were also in flux.

Jeremy had made a big career change a decade previously and was on the cusp of another. Early in his working life, he had been a conference organizer, but he had always harbored a passion for digital visual arts. While wrestling with questions of direction in his mid-forties, he realized that he wanted to make this passion a more central part of his life. Fortunately, the digital visual arts industry was buoyant, and after much hustling and many failed attempts, Jeremy realized his dream and got into this new world. For the next decade, he dedicated himself to a studio. Its main projects were now ending, and Jeremy was considering his next steps. He felt sad to close a chapter of what he knew was a big part of his life's work, but was confident enough at this point to feel freedom and excitement, too, for what might come next.

For her part, Norah had been working for the same small agricultural machinery business for the last twenty-six years and felt, as she put it, "part of the furniture." She appreciated her colleagues and was good at her job, but she had felt stuck for a long time. Although she had always been interested in agriculture, her real passion had been on the people side. She had tried to transition to a job that made better use of her people skills, but had never been able to make it work. Her most concerted effort came at the time when Jeremy moved into digital arts. Like him, she had hit an impasse, and for two years she tried to explore options. She considered retraining as an occupational psychologist, moving to an HR consultancy, and even becoming a teacher. She longed for Jeremy to encourage her to move and be excited about her quest. Jeremy, however, was too caught up in his move, and the pay cut he accepted to pursue his passion meant that Norah could not afford to take time out to retrain if the family was to keep its lifestyle.

Now, Norah's lack of mobility had come back to bite. Three weeks before her mother passed away, she had been asked to take voluntary redundancy wrapped up as an early retirement deal. No longer one of the bright young things, she could see that her skills had eroded. Still, the humiliation of it—she had dedicated her working life to the business and was being thrown on the scrap heap at fifty-seven. She felt disoriented and lost.

From the sofa, Norah and Jeremy could see their backyard. Two house sparrows were pecking at the bird feeder gathering seeds for their young. "Full of purpose," Norah thought, "unlike us."

Alone in the house, children and parents gone, for the first time in almost two decades they had no one to look after except each other. Although touched by grief, Jeremy had a palpable sense of opportunity. They could reinvent themselves, become something new. Make a difference in the world. Start a new journey. Norah, however, was stuck with loss. No career, no parents, no children to care for—who was she now? She could hardly bear facing the question.

The Third Struggle

Faced with role losses and the identity voids that these provoke, couples like Norah and Jeremy are thrown into the struggle of their third transition. The broadened path they crafted during their second one begins to crumble, and the belief that they had figured out what they really wanted falters. As both partners wrestle with questions of identity and purpose, they must revisit the roles they play in each other's lives once more.

The struggle period of the third transition contains traps that can intensify or prolong couples' struggle and hinder their ability to answer the defining question of this final transition: *Who are we now?* The first trap occurs when couples get caught up in unfinished business from their first two transitions. Ingrained relational patterns and agreements that are suboptimal become apparent, and couples must work through these before they can figure out who they want to become for the rest of their lives together. The second trap, narrowing horizons, occurs when couples mentally narrow their options and fail to consider emerging possibilities available to them in this new life period.

How long couples spend struggling, how severe the struggle becomes, and whether they can make it out depends on their ability to overcome these traps and on their ability to become explorers once again.

Trap 1: Unfinished Business

When couples tackle the identity voids of their third transition, be they real or anticipated, they do not work from a blank slate. By this stage in life, they carry habits established during their two previous transitions. Whether they are in a new relationship or one that began decades ago, they swim in a sea of relational patterns, approaches, past decisions, and assumptions that influence how their third transition unfolds. Some of these patterns can help them remain buoyant. For example, you may have developed ways of supporting each other and approaches to life that let you both thrive and overcome challenges together. Some of these patterns, however, drag couples down.

Problematic patterns accumulate when couples fail to resolve the developmental tasks of their previous transitions or don't develop supportive habits along the way. Although couples can move to a new transition without fully resolving the developmental task of a previous one, that unfinished business hinders their progress in the next. That can be true even if you change partners, as we often carry problematic assumptions and habits with us into new relationships, which can hinder the third transition.

How the Second Transition Can Impact the Third

The developmental task of the second transition is mutual individuation—that is, both partners identify and pursue what they each want out of their careers, lives, and relationship. To do this successfully, they must figure out what they really want and then renegotiate the roles they play in each other's lives and the division of career and family labor that they established in their first transition.

As we saw in chapter 7, partners who don't complete the second transition either both become stuck on the path they crafted at the end of their first transition or their paths diverge. One moves to an individuated path, while the other remains stuck. While the one who remains stuck may still be objectively successful—moving up their company's career ladder, for example—they are developmentally trapped on a path that is not truly theirs. It is a success that they do not own.

Unilateral, rather than mutual, individuation often occurs in couples who build an asymmetric secure base relationship during the struggle of their second transition. If you recall from chapter 6, we all need a secure base—someone who encourages us to explore and take risks and at the same time, give us a safe place to retreat to in order to grow. In couples with asymmetric secure base relationships, only one partner plays this role for the other. Typically, the partner who benefits from the secure base transitions to an individuated life path, while the one who provides but does not receive a secure base remains stuck. While some couples can initially bury the effect of this asymmetry, should they make it to their third transition, it inevitably resurfaces.

This is what happened to Norah and Jeremy. During their second transition, Norah had been a secure base for Jeremy. She encouraged him to follow his passion for digital arts and supported him when he got rejected from the first few positions he applied for. She also enthusiastically encouraged him to take the plunge when he eventually found a job in the studio he now worked at, even though his lower salary hurt their finances. Jeremy felt indebted to Norah for her support, yet was unable to reciprocate. He was so caught up in his transition that he had neither the energy nor the inclination to be a secure base for her. He had not taken an active interest in, nor encouraged her to follow, her passion for people skills. Rather, he had subtly encouraged her to stick it out in her job.

The developmental divergence in their paths had caused friction between Norah and Jeremy for a while, but as the years went by, she buried her resentment and the couple moved on. Practically, their family was in good shape. Both partners had steadily progressed in their careers while dedicating themselves to their boys and to each other. The good times, however, could not compensate for the asymmetry left over from their second transition.

As their roles shifted and their third transition began, the asymmetry resurfaced, and they found themselves on opposite ends of an emotional spectrum of sorts. Norah was fixated on the losses they were experiencing, while Jeremy gravitated toward the opportunities. In their second transition, Jeremy had built up his muscles in the art of change. He had become skillful at self-reflection and overcoming rejection and loss, and gained confidence that he could successfully make transitions. Because he had reinvented himself before, when the third transition rolled in, he had the courage to do so again. While their second transition had made Jeremy more open to, excited about, and skillful at change, it had made Norah more closed and fearful of it.

Norah too had experienced loss and rejection during the second transition, but with a lack of support and no positive resolution, both of which made her retreat and shy away from change. She became despondent and resurfaced old resentments toward Jeremy. "He's always trying to shake things up. It's all right for him—he's had a big break. It made him into an over-grown enthusiastic puppy dog. He just can't see how hard it's been for me. How hard it is for me now. He's all about a new start now, but where was he then, fifteen years ago? It's hard for me to get past that."

Jeremy was sympathetic to Norah's feelings, but became easily frustrated with her reactions. "Look, Norah is in a tough spot right now, but we've got to get past that. Right now, she's wallow-ing. There are so many things we could do. I want us to do some blue-sky thinking, reinvent ourselves together. I've tried to snap her out of it, but she keeps coming back to what could have been. It's pretty depressing."

Their polarization led to tension and deadlock. It became ap-parent that the asymmetry that resulted from their second tran-sition had created a gulf between them that they now found hard to bridge. Like other couples I spoke to who carried over asym-metry from their second transition, both Norah and Jeremy knew that they needed to contend with the pressing questions of iden-tity they faced, but until they could build a bridge between their polarized positions, neither could move forward. We'll explore how couples can bridge this gulf in the next section. Before we do so, let's complete the picture by digging into the dynamics we can carry from our first transition.

How the First Transition Can Impact the Third

The developmental task of the first transition is to figure out how you can accommodate each other's lives and careers in a way that enables you both to thrive over the long term. Couples' tendency to rely too heavily on economic decision criteria, focus on the short term, and prioritize practical issues means that they don't always do this accommodation deliberately. And once it's set in motion, many couples don't revisit their accommodation and the agreements they made for decades. If this neglect occurs, then regrets for choices made less than deliberately resurface in the third transition.

Pablo and Sofia met and fell in love in their late forties, during a weekend painting course. Sofia's first husband had died in a car accident when their daughter was only three years old. She had spent the next fifteen years as a single mother, raising her daughter while working as a family lawyer at a small local firm. She prided herself on her career and on her daughter's academic achievements. Now her daughter was on the cusp of attending college, planning to study law like her mother, and Sofia felt that she could finally relax and consider who she wanted to become in this next phase of life.

Pablo's journey to the painting course had been very different. A deeply religious man, he had married young and spent his first decade of married life as a missionary. His wife was the highflier; they had agreed that her diplomatic career would take priority and pay the bills and he would follow her postings seeking missionary work wherever they went. In their mid-twenties, they were posted to the Philippines. Driven by their desire to make a difference in the world, they adopted orphaned twin babies. Pablo became the lead parent, and his missionary calling was firmly relegated to second place. Still, for twenty years, he followed his wife around the world, working in Catholic missions. Then, as their children left home, his wife announced that she was leaving him. Pablo was devastated. He reeled at the implications of divorce, which was outside his belief system, and struggled to get back on his feet. After four years of painful adjustment, he was just beginning to figure out who he was when he met Sofia.

Pablo and Sofia entered their new relationship carrying very different baggage from their first transition. Sofia had been forced by her husband's tragic death to have the lead career and be the sole parent. She was now ready for a change of pace. Pablo had accepted having a secondary career and being the lead parent in his marriage, but when he looked back, he regretted his choices. He felt that he had betrayed his calling and was now eager to make up for lost time. These regrets pushed them in opposite directions as they considered who they wanted to become together. Like many late-love couples, they were simultaneously facing their third transition while redoing their first.

"I have dreams that we'll run a small bed-and-breakfast in the countryside, relax, and be together," explained Sofia. "Getting off the rat race is important to me now. I don't want to dedicate myself too much to work. I have other priorities. We could become a mellowed-out, peaceful couple, and enjoy an outdoorsy life."

Pablo, though, had different plans. "I really want to dedicate myself to a mission for the next decade. There are a couple of residential youth centers looking for new leaders. I think it would be meaningful to do that together. Devote ourselves to something meaningful. Our backgrounds are so complementary; Sophia could run the administration, and I could focus on the social mission. I'm ready to do some real work now."

In many ways, Pablo and Sofia were lucky. They were both keen to build something together and reinvent themselves as individuals and as a couple. But the thrust of their imaginations was very different because of the regrets they carried from their first transitions. Sofia longed to invest less in her career, while Pablo hungered to invest more. Their situation is not uncommon. However, it is often women, not men, who find themselves in Pablo's position, wanting to push harder in the later phase of their careers.

Gender differences in career cycles are rarely discussed in couples, but they are very real. Although trends are rapidly changing for younger generations, in couples who were born in the 1960s and before, it's still most common for the man to take the lead career position and be the secondary parent while the woman takes the secondary career position and is the lead parent. Once this traditional accommodation is adopted, twenty-plus years of adherence to it lands men and women in very different places.

The intensive child-rearing years of the thirties and forties slow down the careers of women who are lead parents but do not necessarily temper their ambition. As their children leave home, these women can have fifteen or twenty years of career ahead of them and are often motivated to accelerate or chart new paths. They may want to become someone different professionally, and it's no surprise that women's careers often peak later than those of men. At the same time, their male partners have been chasing success at full throttle for decades. By the time they experience the identity voids that mark the start of the third transition, their career is likely to be close to its pinnacle; they may be tiring of the rat race and be ready for a very different challenge. Even when both partners are happy with choices they made in their first transition, when they reach their third, leftover regrets—and limited time to make up for them—can pull them in different directions.

Resolving Unfinished Business

Resolving the unfinished business of couples' first two transitions is critical to work through the third. The most difficult baggage to unpack is the asymmetric secure base relationship that some couples, like Norah and Jeremy, develop. Not only does the asymmetry leave partners polarized in their development and in their outlook on the third transition, it also leaves one partner convinced that the other is not committed to their growth. To resolve this asymmetry, couples must acknowledge how they got to where they are and recommit to play new roles for each other in the future.

The many great times that Norah and Jeremy had shared over their years motivated them to tackle their relationship tensions, but it was not easy going. Initially Norah approached the challenge from the position of the victim: "I was filled up with resentment. I think I had suppressed it for a long time and suddenly it all bubbled up at once. I blamed Jeremy for the position I was in, and I resented that he didn't feel the same losses as me." Norah's resentment was met with Jeremy's guilt and frustration. "I did feel bad for Norah. I know I wasn't as supportive as I should have been. But I am also not a villain. It was annoying and hurtful to be put in that box."

Honestly airing their hurt and frustration, Norah and Jeremy slowly came to see that, as Norah put it, "it took two to tango." They acknowledged that they had both contributed to the asymmetry in their own ways. Since her youth, Norah had tended to play the role of the saint in her relationships with friends, family, and loved ones. She constantly made sacrifices that often harmed her, but also gave her a sense of value and self-worth. On his part, Jeremy had got so caught up in his own passion that he had gladly accepted Norah's sacrifice. While on the surface, Norah was the victim and Jeremy the perpetrator, they came to understand that their asymmetry was a mutual creation.

Once they set about remedying their asymmetry, they overcompensated at first. Jeremy went out of his way to become a perfect supporter for Norah and did not ask for anything back. Although Norah enjoyed the support, she was thrust outside her comfort zone because she lost yet another role that she had cherished, after all—being Jeremy's supporter. They slowly readjusted and set about building a mutual secure base relationship. As they did so, the polarization in their positions toward the third transition eased. Norah attuned to the new opportunities they faced and began to share some of Jeremy's excitement. Likewise, Jeremy got more in touch with the losses they were experiencing, and his enthusiasm for the future left space for some mourning of the past.

As Norah and Jeremy's story illustrates, the best way to resolve an asymmetric secure base dynamic is through figuring out and acknowledging how you built it and taking concrete steps to change it. Resolving the career-prioritization regrets that we carry with us from our first transition takes different, albeit no less important, steps. To illustrate, let's return to the story of Zara and Mohammed, whom we met in chapter 8.

Throughout their marriage, Mohammed had always had the primary career and Zara the secondary one. When their children left home, Zara suffered an identity void that dealt a severe blow to her self-esteem. Although she had always found work as an economics researcher in local universities as she followed Mohammed across the world, she lacked a strong sense of professional identity that could compensate for the loss of her active parent identity. Meanwhile, Mohammed was reaching the pinnacle of his career and was ready to kick back. While some men in Mohammed's position are reluctant to let go, having reached the top, Mohammed delighted in the thought of changing pace.

"The solution just seemed obvious," Mohammed explained. "Zara had followed me for many years. And she still had a great career. She had done some really important projects, things I'm very proud of. But she felt lacking somehow, especially after the kids left home. 'Well,' I said, 'now it's your turn to take the lead. I'm happy to follow you wherever, I'll always find things to do.'"

Mohammed's suggestion was just the shock Zara needed. "Mohammed jolted me out of my despair. I realized that my sense of loss was triggered by the children leaving, but that's not really what it was about. I had lost my purpose and direction. When I reevaluated, I thought, 'I'm fifty-three, I have got tons of time to make something of myself.' It was exciting to think about swapping roles."

Zara and Mohammed's solution to resolving the regrets accumulated since their first transition was disarmingly simple. They flipped career-prioritization positions. He could take it easy; she could get the lead. It's not always so straightforward. Often people resist their partner's desire to make up for their regrets, be it reversing positions or meeting on middle ground. It can be both disarming and threatening if your partner announces they want to pull back from the lead career position. Can they afford it? What will they do with their time? It can also be tough when one partner wants both members of the couple to pull back and broaden their horizons but the other still wants to push in their career. If you find yourself with regrets carried over from your first transition, it's important that you map them out together. You might want to revisit the career-mapping exercise I explained in chapter 4 to help you with this task. It is easier if you can resist blaming each other—or yourself—for their existence and focus on how your choices might have generated them and how you can use the years ahead in order to redress them.

For late-love couples like Pablo and Sofia, tackling unresolved career-prioritization regrets carried over from previous relationships can be tricky. Absent a shared history, it's not possible to fall back on a turn-taking decision criterion. As Pablo and Sofia discovered, they needed to wrestle it out. In their case, they decided to follow Pablo's calling and take on the leadership of a Catholic youth center in central Spain. Sophia, however, declined to be a full partner in the endeavor. Instead, she started a part-time law practice in the nearest town and spent the rest of her time enjoying the countryside and encouraging Pablo from the sidelines.

Neither got their perfect dream, but both found contentment in the next stage of life.

Self-Discovery and Reinvention

Once couples have dealt with their unfinished business, they must move on to the main task of the third transition—reinvention. Couples need to manage two self-discovery journeys of sorts, mourning the old and welcoming the new, and then figure out how they fit together and adjust their life path to one that supports who they want to become. Just like the second transition, I have found that couples that successfully work through their third include each other in their reinvention journeys from the get-go. While some of their self-discovery will occur alone or with others, couples that work share their thoughts and feelings along the way and work through this journey together.

The reinvention required in this journey is intimately tied to our changing roles and identity voids: *Who am I now that I am no longer a rising star, a hands-on parent, a caregiving child? And who do I want to become in the next stage of life? How can I make a difference with the time I have left?* Even if you have wrestled with questions of identity before, you must now revisit your previous answers and be open to new ones. The void can bring darkness to your days, but it also makes space for new identities to germinate.

This journey of reinvention takes couples back to the reflection and exploration mode of their second transition. As I detailed in chapter 6, there are many ways we can reflect and explore, and willingness to do so is key. One of the challenges of self-discovery in the third transition is that it requires two willing and curious participants. Both partners must be prepared to play with the idea of who they might become—this aspect of play is a key distinction between the second and third transitions.

Herminia Ibarra, a leading expert on career transitions, and I have written about the difference between working on and playing with our identities.[1] When we work on our identities, we make purposeful moves from A to B. Just like in the second transition, we take time to figure out what B is and then consciously transition to it. Leaving the constraints of A behind is hardly a burden. In contrast, when we play with our identities, we flirt with possibilities and explore multiple options with the purpose of reinvention.

A playful approach is vital for the third transition because people's ambitions and priorities tend to diversify at this stage of life, but what they fear leaving behind is not a constrained but often a cherished self. They must therefore find ways to bring elements of that self with them to ground the new in the cherished accomplishments of the past.

At this stage, self-discovery encompasses but is not restricted to careers. This is a time when people's thoughts also turn to giving back to their community, leaving some kind of legacy, mentoring younger generations, rediscovering passions of their youth, and dedicating themselves more to friendships. The focus is less on *me*, and more on *us*.

Figuring out who you are and who you want to become in light of your history requires you to rethink how to fit love, work, and life together. Fortunately, careers are becoming more flexible, especially for experienced workers, which means that people can more easily combine multiple priorities in ways that were not possible for previous generations. Many of the couples I spoke to who were engaged in self-discovery were latching onto new opportunities that helped them become who they wanted to be as a whole person with others. Here are some options you may want to consider:

> *Retrain and reboot:* With twenty-plus years of working life ahead of them, it's becoming more common for over-fifties to retrain and reboot their careers. Often, this move lets

people tap into interests that have been on the back burner for decades. It can release a reservoir of generative energy that lets us excel in our chosen new directions.

Freelancing: Like Noam, whom we met in chapter 8, more people are becoming freelancers in the third stage of their careers. They have a wealth of expertise and experience, but may have tired of the corporate rat race or reached the most senior position they can. Freelancing is a great way of capitalizing on your skills while buying yourself time and freedom to focus on other interests that run in parallel.

Portfolio careers: People with portfolio careers combine a number of part-time roles at the same time. People often mix and match roles to include freelancing, a part-time role in an organization, and even a pro bono role through which they can contribute to a cause close to their heart. The diversity of portfolio careers can be exhilarating as it lets you pursue multiple ambitions at once.

Entrepreneurship: Although financially risky, the percentage of businesses started by older workers is booming. If you've built up a financial buffer and are feeling up for the challenge, starting a business is an exciting option for the third stage of your careers. It enables you to capitalize on your experience and skills while experiencing the satisfaction of growing something new.

Taking a playful approach to self-discovery and considering new and unusual options to combine work and life is vital to crafting a solid path out of the third transition. To capitalize on these opportunities, both we and our partner need to be open and curious. Which brings us to the second trap of the third transition—narrowed horizons.

Trap 2: Narrowed Horizons

Let's face it. By the time you reach your third transition, you will have likely suffered your fair share of disappointments and setbacks. You may be tired from years of taking care of others or just keeping going on the treadmill. As your roles shift and identity voids expand, the thought of reinvention might be the last thing on your minds.

Although Christoph and Eleanor, whose story I shared in chapter 8, had spent their adult lives striving for the best, when they hit their third transition, their paths diverged. Eleanor saw their changing situation as an opportunity to take it easy and capitalize on everything they had built. She had little interest in self-discovery. Instead, she wanted to push aside the losses she was experiencing and enjoy what she had. Christoph, meanwhile, saw their losses as an opportunity to become someone new. He flung himself into a journey of self-discovery and opened his horizons. He spoke to people who had made late career transitions and tried to figure out who he wanted to become.

At first, Christoph didn't mind that Eleanor's horizons were narrower than his, but the fact that they weren't on the same journey soon caught up with them. "She calls it my 'late midlife crisis,'" he said despondently. "At first, it was a bit of a joke; but I won't deny it, it hurts. I thought I would be able to drag her along on my journey but now I see that all she can do is denigrate it." Eleanor's narrow horizons and lack of curiosity for Christoph's journey was damaging, as was the divergence of their paths. This drift, combined with the gulf of resentments they had built up over the years, was too much for the couple to overcome, and eventually they decided to go their separate ways.

You may not be in such a polarized position as Christoph and Eleanor, with one pushing for self-discovery and the other pushing for the status quo. Many of us simply have no role models for what reinvention looks like at this stage of our lives. When we look to what previous generations have made of the later stage of their careers, it naturally narrows our horizons. Many of us don't seek, or need, major change at this point in our lives, but by narrowing our horizons, we miss opportunities to fill identity voids and renew our life paths. To avoid the trap of narrowed horizons, we need to be curious about each other and willing to self-discover together. We need to become explorers again.

Becoming Explorers Again

Children are brilliant explorers. They are curious about the world, themselves, and those around them. They actively seek new experiences and experiment with what they like and don't like. They rarely take things for granted and constantly ask "Why?" We have the capacity to be explorers at any age, but most of us suppress our childhood curiosity as life progresses and responsibilities build up.

Becoming an explorer again is a life-changing experience at any age and is especially rejuvenating in later life. The shifts in people's roles and identities offer a perfect excuse to question their current work, life, and love and to play with alternatives. Many people associate exploring with looking for new options, which is surely important. But equally, exploring is about questioning our current assumptions and approach and asking, *Is this really how things need to be?"*

It's particularly powerful when two partners become explorers again together. When you are curious not just about your life and work, but your partner's life and work, you can unlock an immense capacity for joint revitalization in your couple. This capacity and its connection to recovering exploration was one of the patterns that struck me most when I spoke to couples in their third transition and beyond. I met many couples who were charting new paths out of their third transition, and these often involved a coming together of interests or work.

A few couples I spoke to, including one we'll meet in chapter 10, took the plunge into combining their love and work at this stage. Working together on entrepreneurial ventures or specific projects in their career portfolio was a way for them to combine interests and build something together. Other couples preferred to keep their shared passions outside the professional domain, but still used their joint exploration to push each other to new heights.

When couples become ensnared in the traps of the third transition and struggle to become explorers again, they face a rocky road. Some, like Christoph and Eleanor, go their separate ways; others resign themselves to a suboptimal path. But once they can unpack the baggage from the past, they can make space for new experiences and identities in the future. In the next and final chapter, we'll meet three couples who became explorers again in their third transition and reinvented their path for the next stage of life.

10

Couples That Work

This chapter tells the stories of three couples that work; that is, couples whose members resolved to share a life and two careers, couples that never settled for the idea that one could either truly love one's work or another person, and couples that did not take their relationship for granted, and did the work it takes to thrive in love and work, together, over a lifetime. By this point, you will have realized that the "work" we are concerned with in this book is not just the work that couples put into their careers. It is the work they put into each other to make it through the struggles and transitions I have described.

The three couples in this chapter, when I talked to them, were enjoying a period of renewal in the final stage of their careers. Each couple faced shifts in their roles that deprived them of valued identities, wrestled with fundamental questions about who they were now, and became explorers again. Through all this, they figured out who they wanted to become.

The three couples have different backgrounds, career trajectories, and life paths. They made different decisions and prioritized different aspects of their lives. They faced different ups and downs, some unexpected, some self-imposed. And they ended up in different places, physically, practically, and personally. What they share is a common approach. Each couple treated loving and working as an art to be mastered through practice and investment, they treated their careers and couples as a labor of love and helped me understand the only real secret of couples that work—for them, labor *is* love. These couples' stories hold important lessons for those of us facing our third transition, and for any of us trying to thrive in love and in work over the course of our lives.

Angela and Robert: In It for the Long Haul

Angela and Robert closed the Skype call and grinned tearfully. "Grandparents!" exclaimed Robert as they dissolved into joyous giggles. "This calls for a celebration."

The news that their eldest daughter, Maria, was expecting their first grandchild topped off three golden years for the soon-to-be Granny and Grandad. Having met in the office while working on the same team in a semiconductor manufacturing plant in Munich thirty-four years ago, they had come full circle and were once again working together as consultants to the same industry. The decision had not been taken lightly, but it had paid off. Their expertise in the industry generated a steady flow of business, and they cherry-picked assignments that interested them. Working four days a week, they earned enough to keep them going and they dedicated one day a week to their own projects.

Robert used his fifth day to pursue his passion for making model airplanes, while Angela volunteered at a center that ran art classes for refugee children. Broadening their horizons had given them satisfaction and meaning. The changes to their working arrangements were accompanied by changes to their living ones. For the first time in thirty-one years, they were both living permanently in the same town. Being together 24/7 took some getting used to, but by the time I met them, they were reveling in each other. I was inspired, and it was not lost on them how fortunate they had been.

"We're rediscovering each other, and I like what I'm finding," said Robert charmingly, "Don't get me wrong—we've had some good times along the way, but these really are golden years."

Angela chimed in, "Yes, times are great, but let's not forget what it's taken us to get here. We're fortunate, but boy, have we worked to get where we are."

Like many couples, Angela and Robert met at work. Angela was twenty-three, a bright-eyed engineering graduate who joined the semiconductor company to learn about what was, at the time, a cutting-edge industry. Robert was twenty-five and already climbing the ranks in the manufacturing plant. He had married his childhood sweetheart at twenty-one, which he called a "youthful mistake," and when he met Angela, he was in the midst of divorcing.

Angela was immediately drawn to Robert's good looks and determined personality, but she knew of his divorce and assumed that he was too troubled to bother with, so she kept her distance. When they were assigned to the same task force, however, Angela caught Robert's eye. "She was a force of nature," he reminisced. "When she walked into a room, you just couldn't help but notice. She was stunning and had a fierce intellect. Honestly, at the beginning I found her intimidating."

Their mutual attraction soon blossomed into an office romance, but their yearlong honeymoon period ended abruptly when Angela unexpectedly became pregnant. "When I first found out, I was frightened. We were a new couple—a young couple. And Robert's divorce was still not finalized. I remember it vividly: Robert was away on a training course and those were the days before cell phones, so I couldn't speak to him. For one sleepless night, I even considered having an abortion and not telling him."

When Robert returned, Angela revealed the news, which, much to her relief, he met with excitement. "I was dead against getting married again, and we never married in all these years, but I was over the moon to be having a baby with Angela. That was really the moment when we fully committed to each other."

Just as they were getting accustomed to the thought of becoming parents, Robert was assigned to a team that would open a new plant more than three hundred miles from their hometown. Little did the couple know that this was the start of three decades in which they would live together for only half that time, interspersed with long periods apart.

As Robert explained, "In those days, you didn't negotiate a promotion. You just took it and went. So we just had to find a way to make it work." The couple abruptly found themselves in their first transition, struggling to figure out how they could structure their lives in a way that allowed them both to thrive at work, maintain a good relationship, and be good parents. Robert had learned the importance of tough conversations from his failed first marriage, so he made sure that he and Angela deliberately figured things out.

"Over the course of a few months, we agreed on a set of principles that we have stuck to ever since," explained Angela:

First was the importance of work. We were both brought up in families with strong Protestant work ethics. It was instilled in us from an early age. Neither of us is particularly ambitious to reach senior management positions, but working and doing work well is incredibly important to both of us. Second was the importance of having independent children. We are not helicopter parents. It was important to us that our children became independent members of society from an early age. Third was our relationship. We agreed that nothing should go unsaid, that we would always share everything.

Having set their three principles deliberately, Angela and Robert entered a relatively stable period. They had three children in six years—Maria, Emma, and Alexander—while Robert commuted, spending the weekends in their hometown of Munich and the weekdays at his workplace in Dresden, an almost five-hour drive away. Their industry's volatility meant that the commuting continued throughout most of their career. Of the years their children lived at home, Robert spent nine working elsewhere, Angela spent four, and for two years both were away during the week. Luckily, both sets of grandparents lived in Munich and devoted themselves to their grandchildren, even living in Angela and Robert's house full-time for the two years that they worked elsewhere.

While they recalled them as very tough, Angela and Robert felt that their first six years made them a couple. They discovered a well of resilience and the joy of supporting each other's careers. One advantage of working for the same company in the same field was that they could help each other practically. They checked each other's reports, strategized about new manufacturing processes, and discussed how to deal with office politics. Work made them feel emotionally close even when they were physically distant.

Angela and Robert's second transition began in their late thirties, when they started questioning what they really wanted from life. Unfortunately, this period of questioning coincided with a downturn that hit their company hard. In the space of four weeks, both of them were laid off. Self-exploration suddenly became a luxury that they could not afford—they needed to put food on the table. Then, just before Angela was due to leave the company, she was offered a job at another site. It was a demotion, and her pay would be cut, but it was a job. She took it without question and supported the family for a year while Robert looked for work.

"It was the lowest point of my life," explained Robert. "I got very down. Work is such a central part of who I am; without it I felt lost. My self-esteem dropped very low." He eventually found work in a smaller firm and the couple entered a decade that they referred to as the "career dark age." The industry took a long time to recover, and the pair hopped between companies to chase work that would build their skills and pay the bills. While they succeeded in keeping the family afloat, neither was able to engage with the existential questions of the second transition, which lingered in the back of their minds.

If their careers were stagnant, however, Angela and Robert's family was blossoming. They now had three independent teenagers, each with their own passions and dreams. They could see that their loving, hands-off parenting had paid off and they enjoyed building the foundations of adult relationships with their brood.

As their youngest, Alexander, flew the nest, the identity questions of the third transition came to the fore. At the same time, questions of direction, unresolved from the second transition, were still lingering. Both Angela and Robert reached an impasse. "We'd never aimed for the top, but we still wanted to be something professionally, and the decade of piecemeal work started to hurt. We had lost our professional identities and our direction along the way," Angela recalled.

At the same time as longing for more, professionally, they began to feel the pull of other priorities. They wanted to invest more in their relationship and make sure that they would never have to live apart again. They were also interested in rekindling lost passions and starting new ones. Angela in particular felt the urge to contribute more to their hometown community in some way. Finally, they wanted to be more supportive of their now-aging parents, to pay them back for all the support they had received over the years.

Being highly practical people, Angela and Robert were unaccustomed to reflecting on themselves and were not quite sure how to "work" on elusive questions of direction and identity. They found it hard to play with possibilities, and each time they sat down to think things through, they ended up trying to map out the future on an Excel spreadsheet. Those spreadsheets, however, never felt as binding as the corporate ones they had once worked together on. The couple grew increasingly frustrated with their failed attempts to make sense of who they wanted to become in the next stage of their lives.

After a year of struggling, boxed in by their narrowed horizons, they found inspiration from an unexpected source—Emma, their middle child. The explorer of the family, Emma could see her parents' impasse. One Christmas break, while back from college, she challenged them to do better. In the way only young adult children can, she bluntly told her parents that they were stuck and too narrow-minded to look at opportunities around them. "It's quite something when your twenty-one-year-old daughter holds up a mirror and shows you how constrained your thinking has become. I have to be honest," admitted Robert, "I didn't like it."

When Emma returned to college, however, her challenge sank in, and Angela and Robert slowly began to become explorers again. They regained curiosity about their lives, each other, and possibilities for their couple. They questioned their long-held assumption that they needed to work in a corporation, and they started to look for more flexible alternatives that would let them use their expertise, have an impact, and rebalance their career with other priorities. They noticed a shift in the industry away from in-house specialists and toward external experts. Although they had never been highfliers, both had good reputations for delivering well-researched, meticulous, and diligent work. Furthermore, years hopping between companies had given them a large network across many of the semiconductor and technology companies in Germany.

With the help of a friend who was a good sounding board, they mapped out ways to build a freelance consulting business. They had paid off their mortgage, were not big spenders, and lived in a country with a solid national health system, so they felt that they could afford the risk of setting up alone. They could turn their children's old bedrooms into offices—all they needed were laptops and telephones. They did hesitate before starting a venture together, but their enjoyment of talking about work and bouncing ideas around gave them the belief that they could make it work. It would let them return to their youthful colleagueship and catch up on all that time spent working apart. Their reinvention was, alas, grounded in their chosen history. Nevertheless, they decided to give it a year's trial period. The rest, some say, is history. But for them, it was a new story, too.

What impressed me most about Angela and Robert was that they never shied away from tough conversations and they constantly invested in working things through. Some of the big choices they made—living apart for long periods, not being helicopter parents, and working together—fly in the face of current trends and advice. In many societies, parents are guilted into believing they need to be ever-present, active parents, and most people would say that living apart over the long term is a relationship killer. Likewise, I've read many well-meaning advice articles and books that claim couples are happiest when they have different career tracks. The stories of couples like Angela and Robert have taught me that, like all the other one-size-fits-all instructions thrown at dual-career couples, these beliefs are simply not correct.

Mind you, the two of them had given important things up, like living together all the time, and wanted to do some catching up; but crucially, they did not regret what they had missed. Why? Because they had sacrificed it, together, for the sake of becoming who they were. It was therefore easier to move to exploration, once past their impasse, because they had unfulfilled wishes, surely, but few regrets. That combination might well be the best position to tackle the third transition and what lies beyond it.

What I learned from Angela and Robert, and many other couples who had different priorities and made different choices, is that it's not *what* you do, but *how* you do it that makes the difference. Clichéd as it might sound, it really is all about the process, not about the specific choices. But you can only trust the process if you've worked hard at it, as Angela and Robert did, from early on. There are a multitude of parenting and relationship approaches, all of which can produce healthy, well-adjusted children and a strong relationship if explicitly negotiated and agreed upon up front. Likewise, and as someone who often works with Gianpiero, my husband, I can attest that while working together may be best avoided for some couples, it can be a highly rewarding route for others.

Li and Mei: The Power Couple

Li and Mei's intense vitality struck me immediately when I first met them. It was a rainy afternoon, and they entered the coffee shop hand in hand, radiating a sense of passion and possibility I had observed in many twenty-something couples during the course of my research. Those were the couples that, I used to think, looked like they had just made love before their interviews. At fifty-eight and fifty-seven, Li and Mei were reinventing their lives and careers on the tail end of their third transition as a couple.

Li and Mei were the most high-ranked business leaders I spoke to during my research—Li the CEO of a retailer, and Mei a board director at a media company. And they had recently been named as a power couple in an international business magazine. Their shiny exterior, however, hid a more tumultuous story.

They had met at the welcome party for their MBA program. Li, an incoming student, described being immediately captivated by Mei, a senior cohort student and one of the party organizers. "She was the life and soul of the party, she must have spoken to literally hundreds of people that night, but I was determined to attract her attention. I knew from the first moment that she was the woman for me." At 1 a.m. Li's determination paid off, and they became a couple shortly thereafter.

Both ambitious and career-oriented, they decided to prioritize their careers over their relationship for the first five years following their graduation. They lived largely separate lives, working long hours to accelerate their careers in different cities and meeting on weekends, often with former classmates from their MBA program. They enjoyed being in a social circle of high-potentials, and it spurred them on to aim higher professionally.

As they hit their mid-thirties, their thoughts turned to settling down, and they faced the first transition. "Getting married was a no-brainer for me. I loved Li and I knew he was the best man for me," explained Mei, "but I was much more ambivalent about children." Mei had witnessed classmates' careers fall off the rails after having children and she did not want to make that sacrifice. Li, however, desperately wanted to start a family and spent months trying to persuade her.

Mei eventually capitulated when Li committed to leaving his job as a management consultant, which saw him constantly on the road, and getting a more stable corporate job, which would allow him to actively co-parent their children. They married, moved in together, and became pregnant with twins all in the space of five months. Mei and Li were highly organized, and as Mei's belly grew, they built an intricate plan for how they could make their careers and new babies fit together. On the day of the birth, they confidently made their way to the hospital ready to tackle the next chapter of their lives.

Then the unthinkable happened. One of their twins became distressed and died during delivery. "Everyone says that losing a child is the worst thing that can possibly happen to you. I would say 'Don't even try to imagine it,'" reflected Li. "It was traumatic in every sense of the word. And so, so confusing. We had this beautiful, perfectly healthy baby girl in our arms whom we were head over heels in love with and so happy to have, and at the same time we had to make funeral arrangements for her sister. The grief combined with the joy was too much."

As straight-A students, graduates of Ivy League colleges, and people who had known only career success, Li and Mei had never before faced serious setbacks in life. Now they faced unimaginable loss. Consumed by grief, they began to question everything. "Our daughter was so, so precious that we became paranoid about everything. Was the nanny we'd chosen good enough? Should we be the ones who care for her full-time? And after all that had happened, where was the meaning in our careers? Everything was up in the air," reflected Mei.

With the help of a grief counselor, the couple slowly got back on their feet. Li began his new job in the corporate world, and after five months, Mei returned to work. Grief ebbed and flowed; it remained a part of their lives, but they were determined to get back to living fully—even with it—for the sake of Julia, their bubbly little girl.

Li and Mei's first transition began with tragedy but followed a pattern familiar to other early-stage couples. They struggled to put their well-organized plan for making it work into action. Both partners' jobs involved travel, and they fought often about whose should get priority. They also bickered about the best way to bring up Julia, each believing their way was best and subtly derogating the other's parenting style. Their first three years as parents, in short, were tense.

A reunion weekend with former MBA classmates, many of whom were at a similar life stage, however, led to a break-through. The group of friends honestly and openly shared their struggles, and each couple discussed their attempts to overcome them. Mei and Li realized that they had been fighting about the day-to-day problems without trying to solve their underlying issues. Whose career had priority? And what kind of parents did they want to be? How could they free Julia from the burden of their anxiety about making sure that she never struggled in life? After much discussion, they agreed on a double-primary career model. They agreed to both limit their travel to 10 per-cent of their time; only pursue career options in New York, their adopted hometown; and let their parents be more actively in-volved in caring for Julia, something they had resisted until that point.

What followed were seven years of stability, growth, and ad-venture. Happy in their newfound rhythm, Li and Mei's careers accelerated. Both were promoted to their first senior management roles and they excelled. At the same time, they enjoyed parenting a growing child. They rejoiced in Julia's curiosity, in weekend trips to museums and animal parks, and in holidays on the coast with grandparents. Life was busy and rewarding.

Their second transition began at a time when the startup world was booming. By this stage, Li and Mei were in their mid-forties and on the cusp of their first senior executive roles. Their suc-cess, however, made them question what else they could do in life. "We'd spent all our careers making money for someone else. We had the skills and the knowledge, and both of us wanted to run something for ourselves. The startup world was very appealing, especially because a lot of our friends were transitioning at that time and some were enjoying big successes," explained Li.

Carried along by the wave, both decided to look for options in the startup world. Li was invited to join a team launching an e-commerce business for high-end fashion. The salary was next to nothing, but the stock options that came with the CEO role that Li was offered made it hard to resist. Not that he tried hard to—his move meant that Mei would have to delay hers because the couple needed the steady income from her corporate job, but growth prospects were high for Li's startup and the pair estimated that she would be able to leave her company a year to eighteen months later.

Eighteen months turned into three years of carrying the family as both the primary breadwinner and the primary parent. "The startup was all-consuming," lamented Mei. "For three years, Li took no holidays, worked every weekend and most evenings too. It was brutal. Each time it looked as if the company was about to take off, they faced another setback. I tried to hunker down, but by the end of that period, I was totally burned-out."

After three years, the business ended in what Li described as "soul-crushing failure." Not only did it fold, but Li and Mei lost a large chunk of their savings, which they had invested in the company. Riddled with guilt, Li immediately accepted the first corporate job that came his way, and Mei resigned from hers. She took a six-month career break to recuperate while Li powered through. Just as she was getting back on her feet, she was offered her first executive board position.

It was a big jump, and Mei still harbored dreams of taking a different path. However, Li's experience in the startup world had left them burned, and this new role would offer her a level of influence that she aspired to. With Li's encouragement, she took the plunge and her career soared. Li's work was also back on track, and they entered what Mei referred to as "the most exciting period of our careers. We enjoyed a huge amount of external recognition and we got high on that. Too high. We dropped the ball at home and could only see it when Julia was diagnosed with anorexia."

Julia's diagnosis was "a knife in the stomach," Li admitted, "I have never in my life felt so guilty. We had already lost one daughter and now our hubris was putting our second at risk." The couple immediately scaled back their working hours, and they started family therapy. It was a long road to recovery, but by Julia's sixteenth birthday, she was back on her feet. To celebrate, the family took a two-week cruise in the Caribbean to relax, have fun, and, on Julia's request, plan her strategy to get into college.

"As any parent can attest, getting your child into the college of their choice is no mean feat," said Mei, "Two years of college visits, [studying] for the SAT, and completing college applications went by in a flash and then suddenly it was just us."

Julia's departure hit them hard. For the first time in their lives, they felt without purpose. They realized that since Julia's birth, they had been on an incessant treadmill of activity, partly because of their career drive and partly in response to the death of their second daughter. They had dealt with grief through action and through doting on their precious child, and now it came back like a wave crashing over them. Their third transition began with a vengeance.

"This time, we knew we had to process it," said Li "and it was more than the grief. It was hard to admit it, but we had somehow lost ourselves along the way." Twenty-five years of striving had left little time for their relationship. "We had turned into machines," Mei said, "and in the process had forgotten how to just be together." They saw a distance between them that they needed to bridge. Drifting apart was a realistic possibility.

Li and Mei were fortunate to have earned high salaries throughout most of their working lives, and their modest upbringings, combined with the startup failure, had made them financially prudent. Their savings gave them the opportunity to take a year's sabbatical to take stock and reassess. They had a luxury that few couples can afford—the ability to dedicate themselves 100 percent to answering the defining question of the third transition: *Who do we want to become?*

"It was the most amazing year, and the start of a whole new chapter for us," Li told me. They spent six months working on charity projects in China, their country of origin; took two months of holiday; and spent the remaining four months at home on what Mei described as a "journey of rediscovery." They hired a coach to help them think through the next phase of their lives, attended training courses, and spent a lot of time talking things through together and with friends and acquaintances in their network.

They were almost embarrassed to realize that both of them quietly shared the vision of rebalancing their lives, although both assumed that the other wanted to push on. They wanted to contribute more to their communities at home and in China, and mentor young people so that they could enjoy the business success that they had had. But first, they both wanted one last shot at a big corporate role, a chance to leave their mark on an organization before they transitioned to portfolio careers.

I met them shortly afterward, a CEO and board director thriving in their last big roles and sailing toward the five-year limit they had given themselves to transition to a balanced life and portfolio career that would take them to their sixtieth decade.

Li and Mei worked through the struggle period of their third transition in a way that few can afford—a yearlong sabbatical, a personal coach, and training courses. Their approach, if not their means, however, is far more affordable and worth learning from. First, they purposefully did things that broadened their horizons. Working on new projects, returning to their roots, and going into learning mode are things we can all do. Volunteering or participating on side projects on weekends and evenings, reflecting on our origins and their place in our lives, and learning through books, internet courses, and other sources are options we can all pursue. Second, they dedicated a lot of time to talking things through and getting feedback. They did it together and with others.

The reason I find Li and Mei's story insightful, and the reason I wanted to share it in this chapter, is that it helps to shatter the myth of the so-called power couple. We read a lot about power couples in the press, and it's hard not to either feel envious of their seemingly perfect lives or feel depressed that our own measure up short. Gianpiero once bought me a framed cartoon with the caption "Never compare your inside to someone else's outside" that now hangs on my office wall. While I look at it each working day, I still fall into the trap of believing so-called power couples have everything sorted and in control—that they have it all. As Li and Mei's story shows, scratch beneath the surface and you see that power couples' lives are in fact very similar to the rest of ours. Li and Mei were blessed with intellect and supportive families. They had determination and grit in spades. From their late youth, they had material resources that few of us have. Nevertheless, they faced similar challenges, psychologically speaking, to the rest of us.

Having been publicly named a power couple, I was interested in how Li and Mei reacted to the label. "When people call us that, I feel put on an unrealistic pedestal," reflected Mei. "I mean, we're a very ordinary couple who have had ups and downs like any couple, but it's hard for people to see that. There is this expectation that we're perfect. I struggle to get across to people that, no, we have had big failings just like anyone else."

Li added, "I do recognize that we have enjoyed fabulous objective success, and there was a point when that was really important to me. Ironically, that was the point when subjectively we were failing. Julia was sick, we were miserable, our relationship was on the rocks. Now we're on the cusp of leaving those really high-profile roles. Trust me, no one will call us a power couple in three years' time. But now I actually feel successful in myself, we're in a great space as a couple, Julia is thriving, and we have a clear direction."

Hilke and Sergei: Making Late Love Work

At fifty-two and forty-nine, Hilke and Sergei had long given up on finding love. Hilke had been a journalist for her home country's most respected broadcasting company since her mid-twenties, and she had never been in a long-term relationship. One hundred percent dedicated to her career, she had spent her adult life traveling between war zones and reporting on some of the most brutal conflicts the world has seen in recent times. She became a journalist because she saw it as her calling. This sense of calling made it easy for her to accept the relatively modest salary she had earned throughout her career.

"I didn't own a house, a car, or any of the usual trappings of adult life. I could fit all of my possessions into two big travel bags. I was a nomad." Hilke went on to describe how she had had a series of short-lived relationships in her late twenties and early thirties but could never get through the first transition and craft an interdependent life with someone. "Dating a war correspondent is not exactly a bag of fun, and I've never been willing to compromise on my work, so I just gave up on the idea of marriage and all that. I never wanted to have children, so I don't feel I missed out there. I had my fair share of passionate flings over the years, and that was good enough for me."

Sergei married young. For the first two years, his wife accompanied him as he traveled as a field officer for the UN's water

217

agency. Sergei was an engineer who specialized in designing and building low-cost water-treatment facilities in developing countries. Like Hilke, he saw his work as a calling and was happy to forgo a big salary and a comfortable living to make a difference in the world. When his wife became pregnant with their first child, they decided that she should move back to their hometown outside St. Petersburg, Russia. They bought a small apartment, and Sergei returned home for a few weeks every three months, while his wife did the lion's share of the parenting.

Two children and ten years later, their relationship had become strained to the point of breaking. Sergei's wife gave him an ultimatum—either he returned home and got a permanent job in Russia or she was filing for divorce and would request full custody of their children. "I agonized, but I knew that I would die if I wasn't in the field. My heart is out in the world, solving problems, not in Russia being a family man. It was hard, but I agreed to divorce." Estranged from his ex-wife and two children, Sergei adopted the nomadic life that Hilke knew so well. After his failed relationship, he shied away from forming new attachments and lived a largely celibate life for the next fifteen years.

Hilke and Sergei met in a hotel bar in Kigali, Rwanda. Hilke had returned there to write a series of articles to mark the twentieth anniversary of the end of the genocide that she had covered as a young Austrian war correspondent. Sergei had been based in the city for six months, working on a network of rural water treatment plants two hours away.

"Look—I am a Russian guy, a very rational guy. But honestly, if you asked me that night, I would say that Cupid was in that bar with us."

Sergei and Hilke connected and fell in love. Within three weeks, they had decided to commit to each other for the long term. "There are all sorts of rational explanations I have," explained Hilke. "We were both at natural transition points, considering the next phases of our lives. We were at a point in our lives when we were more open to each other. But the truth is, we fell in love. I found my soul mate. It took fifty-two years, but I was 100 percent certain that we were meant to be together."

The new couple decided to make Athens their home base. After the Greek financial crisis, they could just about afford an apartment on the coast outside the city, and living was cheap. It was also one of the European cities closest to the Middle East and Africa, where the two did most of their work. They returned to their new home at least once a month, and both enjoyed an unexpected transformation.

Hilke experienced what she described as an "opening of my soul" over the next three years. For the first time in her life, she was interested in more than her reporting. And it wasn't just her interest in Sergei and their love. "I discovered a passion for open-water swimming. Each morning, we swim before breakfast—even in the winter we swim. We can walk out of our apartment and straight into the sea. It's hard to explain, but it opened my mind and body to a whole new world in the water. I also returned to writing poetry, something I hadn't done since college." Alongside these new and rekindled passions, Hilke found that love impacted her work, but not in the way she had expected.

"The reason I shied away from relationships for so long was that I believed they would damage my work. I thought I wouldn't be able to write, to report, if I wasn't 100 percent focused. What happened with Sergei was the opposite. My work got better. Being in love with this amazing man opened my heart, and I could report the human side of war zones in a way that I couldn't before. I was able to connect to people in a different way, a more real way, and my reporting reached a new level, a deeper level, if you can understand that."

Hilke and Sergei took an active interest in each other's work, and the impact their relationship had on Hilke's work was mirrored in Sergei. Although he had always felt that his work was a calling, his enthusiasm had started to wane. Once he got together with Hilke, however, he felt his passion and energy return. "My work was more important to me and less important at the same time. I had all sorts of ideas, I wanted to do new things. But it wasn't 100 percent of who I was anymore. I would say that I am now more involved and more detached. I think Hilke has made me better at my job." Like Hilke, Sergei found his interests broadening beyond the calling that had been his obsession for the last twenty-five years, and for the first time the thought of retirement did not fill him with dread.

Hilke and Sergei's journey into love coincided with their third transition. As Hilke noted, they had both begun to face the question of who they wanted to become in the next phase of life. They sensed that their lifestyles were not going to last, and they had little else to fill the identity void that stopping would open. The difference was that they now faced the question together. Naturally curious people, and with little unfinished business from previous transitions, their struggle was more of what Hilke called a "transformation and opening up" than a working through. As they looked out to their last working decade, both had a renewed commitment to their callings and a strong sense that when their careers came to an end, they would embrace the next chapter without many regrets.

Although Hilke and Sergei's story is unique, I chose to share it here because it challenges the common belief that the best dual-career couples can hope for is to negotiate a set of compromises that minimize damage to each other's careers and keep their love alive. Hilke and Sergei, and many other couples whose stories I collected, found that their relationship helped them become who they are. They weren't thriving in their work in spite of their love, but because of it. And they weren't becoming who they wanted to be by working around their partner, but by working with their partner. Their success was enhanced by their relationship, and did not come at the cost of it.

Whenever I think of Hilke and Sergei, I am reminded of a quote by Leo Tolstoy: "One can live magnificently in this world if one knows how to work and how to love, to work for the person one loves and to love one's work." Having spent most of their adult lives believing that their work was incompatible with love, Hilke and Sergei discovered through late love how to live, love, and work magnificently.

The Art of Loving and Working

My favorite book about love is psychoanalyst Eric Fromm's *The Art of Loving*.[1] Fromm uses *loving*, not *love*, in the title to argue that love is a craft learned and developed and practiced every day. There is no love, only loving, and those who are good at loving treat it like an art to be honed, enjoyed, and used. Fromm wrote his masterpiece in the 1950s, a time when the term *dual-career couple* had not been coined, and love and work were usually split. Men were responsible for work, and women cared about love. Today, most men and women are trying to do both well. We no longer strive to master either loving or working. We strive to master loving and working. We strive to combine them in a way that lets us *and* our partners thrive in love *and* work.

In the process of researching and writing this book, I learned that to combine love and work is an art in itself. There are no shortcuts. There are no career hacks. There are definitely no love hacks. There is neither a bullet-point list of tips that will guarantee success nor any one-size-fits-all prescription that will ensure fulfillment. The lack of such prescriptions might disappoint some readers, particularly in light of the current trend of "thought leaders" dispensing neatly packaged solutions to pressing problems. What I've tried to offer here, instead, is guidance on an approach to thriving in love and work.

A quote widely attributed to Sigmund Freud says that "love and work are the cornerstones of our humanness." There is no written record of it in Freud's published work. The closest words he wrote were that "the communal life of human beings had, therefore, a two-fold foundation: the compulsion to work, which was created by external necessity, and the power of love."[2] Freud's view was prescient. The dilemma dual-career couples face today is that we want to thrive in both love and work, yet one of those endeavors—work—is overvalued by the external world, and the other—love—is immensely powerful, yet often undervalued by that world. When was the last time someone congratulated you for being successful in love?

The discrepancy between how we value love and work is easy to deny. "Who says they wished they worked more on their death-bed?" we cry. Of course, love is more important. We may believe this, but few of us act on this belief. Work cannot love you back, we reason. But that is no reason to dismiss it either. The truth is, work gives many of us a sense of meaning and fulfillment. To deny that is to deny our humanness. The discrepancy between how we value love and work also leads us to view the two as antagonistic. If we succeed in one, surely the other will suffer, we reason. Our logic turns our love and our work into a zero-sum game. It doesn't have to be this way.

Couples that work approach the challenges of being in a dual-career couple as an art. How can we do it? First, we must acknowledge that loving and working are both important to our soul, and act on that knowledge. They bring us different joys and make different demands, but they are both vital pieces of our lives and we must balance the value we place on each.

Second, we must make an active choice, every day, to invest in both. I use the word *invest* purposefully. When we invest in something, we devote our time and energy to it with the goal of it appreciating in value. In love, investment includes giving our partner our undivided attention, embracing difficult conversations, being kind in our relationship, enjoying an active sex life, and keeping our partner in mind. This investment yields a strong, fulfilling, and ever-deepening relationship. In work, investment includes striving to give our best work and helping others around us to do the same, searching for the professional path that aligns with our calling rather than the expectations of others, and continuously learning new things and developing ourselves. This investment yields an interesting, fulfilling, and meaningful career.

Third, we need to devote ourselves to becoming better in the practice of love and work. We need to be hungry to learn better ways to love and better ways to work. Like artists, we must never fool ourselves into believing we have cracked the loving and working code; instead we always search for ways to improve, to hone our art. Finally, we need to do all of this together. Because the art of loving and working is not one we can master alone, its very nature means that it can only be mastered together.

Gianpiero and I provocatively entitled our first joint speech "Doing It Together" (and for a few months, that was also the working title of this book). MBA students at INSEAD had invited us to speak about our journey as a dual-career couple and draw lessons from our experience as well as my research that might help them in their careers. As we prepared the speech, it was easy to put ourselves in the shoes of the audience. We met and became a couple as I finished my MBA program. "Let's move to Zurich," suggested Gianpiero on our second date. "Let's take six months and just focus on our relationship. Look, if you accept a job at one of the consultancies you are talking to, you wouldn't think twice of investing six months in a work project. Let's invest in us instead." I said yes—I was so besotted I would have said yes to moving to the South Pole with this man.

A few weeks later, we sat on a rocky beach in Sicily, wrapped up against the December wind, with a bottle of wine, two glasses, a notepad, and two pens. We did the same thing that we have done hundreds of times at work, this time in love. We wrote down and shared what we wanted from our relationship and concerns we had. Over the course of a long and winding conversation, we agreed that if push came to shove, we would sacrifice our work for our love. We too, it seemed, bought into the zero-sum game.

As 2004 turned to 2005, we moved into a small apartment in Zurich with cheap Ikea furniture and overly expensive wine glasses. It turned into an eighteen-month honeymoon. We worked and studied a lot together. I applied to PhD programs, and Gianpiero looked for jobs, and mainly, to borrow a line from Eric Fromm, we stood in love.

That was a long time ago. We have had full-time jobs for over a decade, and children, and far more commitments than we had ever imagined we could hold back then. We had each other, a little money, a few friends, and many big dreams. It still distresses me, at times, that I look back to that as an act of courage, putting our careers aside in our late twenties—well, mine—to treat love as a project worth investing in. It should not be so brave. Or maybe it always should be, lest love loses the magic that no book can reveal.

Who Are We Now?

NATURE OF THE TRANSITION

Fill the identity void left by the loss of significant roles crafted in the first two transitions.

TRIGGERS

Role shifts—such as becoming the most experienced workers, the empty-nester parents, and being seen as the older generation—that result in identity voids with feelings of loss but also opportunity.

DEFINING QUESTION

Who are we now?

Couples must mourn the losses of their shifting roles and welcome the new opportunities they bring, then adjust their life path to one that supports who they want to become.

TRAPS

Getting caught up in unfinished business of the first two transitions

Mentally narrowing your horizons and failing to consider emerging opportunities

RESOLUTION

Grounded reinvention occurs when couples play with the idea of who they might become given their new ambitions and priorities and then reinvent themselves in a way that is grounded in past accomplishments, while opening possibilities for the future.

TOOLS

Shared passions: Develop a joint interest or goal to create a serial space for your couple to thrive (chapter 8)

REFLECTIONS

Becoming explorers again: Tips on developing a mindset that can unlock a capacity for joint revitalization in your couple (chapter 9)

APPENDIX

Studying Dual-Career Couples

In the summer of 2011, Gianpiero and I packed up our house in France, crammed as much as we could into four over-sized suitcases, and boarded a flight to Boston with our two (then small) children in our arms. We were off to spend a year at Harvard Business School, Gianpiero as a visiting professor and I a postdoctoral fellow. As we adjusted to our new world, I became hooked on following the social narratives I encountered in the US media. It was the period following Sheryl Sandberg's landmark Ted Talk, "Why We Have Too Few Women Leaders," which sparked the book *Lean In*. One of Sandberg's famous catch-phrases, "The most important career decision you will make is who you marry," caught the collective imagination. I could hardly disagree with Sandberg's sentiment. But while the role of intimate relationships in people's career was hotly debated in the media, I could find no empirical research that shed much light on it.

My weeks sitting in the Baker library, trawling through electronic databases, revealed a wealth of research on work-life balance and the division of household labor, a stream of work on when and why women opt out of the labor market, and a handful of papers on when and why couples prioritize their careers. While fascinating, none of these answered the questions that interested me. When and how, exactly, are our partners a career asset (for lack of a better word), and when do they become a burden? Was it just a matter of picking Mr. or Ms. Right and "lean in" ever after, or was combining love and work a more complex, relational, and ongoing effort? How do two careers combine over time? My personal interest, its resonance with many professionals I met, and the lack of research led me to embark on a multiyear study of dual-career couples.

The Research Sample

The study that forms the basis of this book is a major extension of a research project on dual-career couples that I worked on with Otilia Obodaru, a professor of organizational behavior at the University of Bath. In that study, we aimed to uncover how partners in dual-career couples shape the development of each other's professional identities and how they experience and interpret the relationships between those identities. While working on this project, I became fascinated by wider questions of how dual-career couples develop over time, what challenges they face, and how their relationships affect their careers and vice versa. As my work with Otilia came to a close, I branched out on my own to gather the stories of a broader range of couples.

I recruited couples for this study through three main sources—the alumni network of INSEAD, the business school where I have been a professor since 2012, personal recommendations from people in my network, and through people reaching out to me directly once they learned about my work. As Joy Pixley—another scholar who has researched dual-career couples—recommends, I identified dual-career couples first by asking them to self-identify as dual-career.[1] I then verified that they had careers—that is, that they had sequences of jobs that "require a high degree of commitment and that have a continuous development character"— by checking their résumés.[2]

My sample selection was not random. It was based on the principle that qualitative social scientists call "theoretical sampling." Similarly, my analysis of the interview data followed the well-established "constant comparison method."[3] In line with this approach, my data collection and analysis went hand in hand. As my research progressed, I constantly recruited new couples to join my sample, comparing and contrasting them to the ones I had already interviewed to see where there were gaps in terms of career type, level of ambition, family situation, age, and length of relationship. I added new couples to fill these gaps as I progressed in my data collection.

I collected the stories of 113 couples. Individuals in the sample ranged from twenty-six to sixty-three years of age, with an average age of forty-four. The majority of couples, seventy-six in total, were in their first significant partnership; the remaining thirty-seven were in their second or subsequent partnership. Individuals in the study came from thirty-two countries on four continents, and their ethnic and religious backgrounds reflected this diversity. At the time of the study, roughly 35 percent of couples resided in North America, 40 percent of couples were based in Europe and 25 percent of couples in the rest of the world. In sixty-eight couples, at least one of the partners had children. One hundred and two of the couples identified as straight, and eleven as gay. Although I did not limit my sampling by sexual or gender orientation, the final sample did not include any couples in which one or both partners identified as transgender. Just under 60 percent of the people in my sample pursued careers in the corporate world. The remaining 40 percent were spread roughly equally between members of the professions, such as medicine, law, and academia; entrepreneurs; public servants; and people working in the nonprofit sector.

Interview Methods

I first interviewed the members of a couple separately and assured each person that the context of our conversation would be kept confidential, including from their partner. This agreement allowed them to speak freely and me to compare partners' stories to each other. Following separate interviews, some couples requested a joint interview, to which I always agreed.

I based my interview on the life-story method and asked people to describe the history of their couple from the time they met through to the future as they imagined it unfolding.[4] The topics we discussed ranged from the couple and its development, the careers of each partner and their development, interactions between careers and couple, and the couple's family and friend network, to name but a few. For people who were in their second or subsequent partnership, I asked similar questions about previous couple relationships.

The interviews were open-ended and usually began with the question, "Tell me the story of how you met your partner." Most interviews lasted two hours or more, with a range from one to four hours. In many cases, I followed interviews up with email exchanges to keep track of the interviewees' stories. All interviews were recorded and transcribed.

I complemented my sample of dual-career couples with interviews with heads of people strategy at thirty-two organizations in tech, health care, professional services, and other industries. These gave me insight into how organizations were thinking about and adapting (or not) to the growing numbers of dual-career couples in the workforce. I also conducted many shorter informal interviews with my executive students at INSEAD who were wrestling with dual-career issues, fellow academics who studied similar phenomena, and human resource professionals. To verify my findings, I gave presentations and conducted workshops for people in dual-career couples, in which I gathered more stories and points of view. All of this supplemental work helped to refine my thinking and the model I developed and presented in this book.

Analyzing the Interviews

My objective in this study was to build theory, not test it. I followed an inductive grounded theory development process that allowed for themes and patterns to emerge from the data.[5] As I described above, I collected data and analyzed the interviews concurrently. As themes emerged from my early data analysis, I subtly adjusted my interview protocol for future interviews to probe them.

I treated each couple as a separate case that could confirm or disconfirm the patterns and conceptual insights that were emerging from my study. I always began my analysis of a couple by reviewing the interview transcript of each partner separately to search for themes and categories that reflected similarities across participants in general and across participants in similar career and life stages more specifically. I then reviewed the interview transcripts of both partners side by side to analyze the couple at the dyadic level. This involved searching for (dis)agreement between how partners described particular events or turning points.

After interviewing and analyzing the transcripts of roughly thirty couples, the categories of the three transitions began to emerge. As they did, I used the theoretical sampling approach I described above to make sure I had enough couples in each transition, and on the paths between them, to make meaningful comparisons and deepen my theorizing.

At this stage, I used an iterative process of moving back and forth between my data, my emerging theory, and the relevant literature on identity, adult development, relationships, attachments, and organizational behavior. This process allowed me to deepen my analysis, refine my theoretical model, and select new couples to include in my sample. The result—after five years of data collection, analysis, theory building, and writing—is this book. I hope you have enjoyed it, and that it helps your couple work!

NOTES

Chapter 1

1. Pew Research Center, *Raising Kids and Running a Household: How Working Parents Share the Load*," Social and Demographic Trends, 2015, http://www.pewsocialtrends.org/2015/11/04/raising-kids-and-running-a-household-how-working-parents-share-the-load/; Office for National Statistics, *Families and the Labour Market, England: 2017*, https://www.ons.gov.uk/employmentandlabourmarket/peopleinwork/employmentandemployeetypes/articles/familiesandthelabourmarketengland/2017#employment-rate-for-mothers-increased-by-118-percentage-points-over-the-past-2-decades; and G. Cory and A. Stirling, *Who's Breadwinning in Europe? A Comparative Analysis of Maternal Breadwinning in Great Britain and Germany* (London: Institute for Public Policy Research, 2015), https://www.ippr.org/files/publications/pdf/whos-breadwinning-in-europe-oct2015.pdf.

2. A. Shimazu, K. Shimada, and I. Watai, "Work–Family Balance and Well-Being among Japanese Dual-Earner Couples: A Spillover–Crossover Perspective," in *Contemporary Occupational Health Psychology: Global Perspectives on Research and Practice*, vol. 3, ed. L. Stavroula and R. R. Sinclair (New York: Wiley, 2014), 84–96.

3. S. Meers and J. Strober, *Getting to 50/50: How Working Parents Can Have It All* (Jersey City, NJ: Viva Editions, 2013).

4. P. Amato and F. Rivera, "Paternal Involvement and Children's Behavior Problems," *Journal of Marriage and Family* 61, no. 2 (1999): 375–384; and E. Cooksey and M. Fondell, "Spending Time with His Kids: Effects of Family Structure on Fathers' and Children's Lives," *Journal of Marriage and Family* 58, no. 3 (1996): 693–707.

5. N. Chethik, *VoiceMale: What Husbands Really Think about Their Marriages, Their Wives, Sex, Housework, and Commitment* (New York: Simon & Schuster, 2006).

6. L. Price Cooke, "'Doing' Gender in Context: Household Bargaining and Risk of Divorce in Germany and the United States," *American Journal of Sociology* 112, no. 2 (2006): 447–472.

Notes

7. US Department of Labor, Bureau of Labor Statistics, *Number of Jobs, Labor Market Experience, and Earnings Growth Among Americans at 50: Results from a Longitudinal Study*, news release, 2017, https://www.bls.gov/news.release/pdf/nlsoy.pdf; J. Meister, "The Future of Work: Job Hopping Is the 'New Normal' for Millennials," *Forbes*, August 14, 2012, https://www.forbes.com/sites/jeannemeister/2012/08/14/the-future-of-work-job-hopping-is-the-new-normal-for-millennials/#4fc9009713b8; and A. Doyle, *Bureau of Labor Statistics (BLS): There's No Better Place Than the BLS to Explore Job and Career Information*, https://www.thebalance.com/how-often-do-people-change-jobs-2060467.

8. A. Gini, *My Job, My Self: Work and the Creation of the Modern Individual* (New York: Routledge, 2000).

9. E. Erikson, *Childhood and Society* (New York: W. W. Norton & Co, 1950).

10. D. Levinson, *The Seasons of a Man's Life* (New York: Ballantine Books, 1978); D. Levinson, *The Seasons of a Woman's Life* (New York: Ballantine Books, 1997); and R. Kegan, *The Evolving Self: Problem and Process in Human Development* (Cambridge, MA: Harvard University Press, 1982).

11. J. E. Pixley, "Career Prioritizing in Dual-Earner Couples," in *Women, Feminism, and Femininity in the 21st Century: American and French Perspectives*, ed. B. Mousli and E. A. Roustang-Stoller (New York: Palgrave Macmillan, 2009), 79–105.

12. S. Stossel, *My Age of Anxiety: Fear, Hope, Dread, and the Search for Peace of Mind* (New York: Knopf, 2014).

Chapter 2

1. R. M. Kreider and R. Ellis, "Number, Timing, and Duration of Marriages and Divorces: 2009," Household Economic Studies, US Census Bureau, Current Population Reports, 2011, https://www.census.gov/prod/2011pubs/p70-125.pdf; and D. Rotz, "Why Have Divorce Rates Fallen? The Role of Women's Age at Marriage," *Journal of Human Resources* 51, no. 4 (Fall 2016): 961–1002.

2. R. Kegan and L. Lahey, *Immunity to Change: How to Overcome It and Unlock the Potential in Yourself and Your Organization* (Boston: Harvard Business Press, 2009).

3. S. Iyengar, *The Art of Choosing* (Boston: Little, Brown, 2010).

4. D. W. Winnicott, *The Collected Works of D. W. Winnicott*, ed. L. Caldwell and H. Taylor Robinson (Oxford: Oxford University Press, 2017); and J. Bowlby, *A Secure Base: Clinical Applications of Attachment Theory* (Abington, UK: Routledge, 1988).

Notes

5. J. Gottman, *The Seven Principles for Making Marriage Work: A Practical Guide from the Country's Foremost Relationship Expert* (New York: Harmony Books, 2000).

6. Gottman, *The Seven Principles*.

7. T. N. Radbury and F. D. Fincham, "Attributions in Marriage: Review and Critique," *Psychological Bulletin* 107, no. 1 (1990): 3–33.

8. J. H. Fowler and N. A. Christakis, "Cooperative Behavior Cascades in Human Social Networks," *Proceedings of the National Academy of Sciences of the United States of America* 107, no. 12 (2010): 5334–5338.

9. J. M. Gottman, *Why Marriages Succeed or Fail: And How You Can Make Yours Last* (New York: Simon & Schuster, 1994).

Chapter 3

1. K. Weisshaar, "From Opt Out to Blocked Out: The Challenges for Labor Market Re-entry After Family-Related Employment Lapses," *American Sociological Review* 83, no. 1 (2018): 34–60; S. A. Hewlett, L. Sherbin, and D. Forster, "Off-Ramps and On-Ramps Revisited," *Harvard Business Review*, June 2010; S. A. Hewlett et al., *Off-Ramps and On-Ramps Revisited* (New York: Center for Work-Life Policy, 2010).

2. P. Stone and M. Lovejoy, "Fast-Track Women and the 'Choice' to Stay Home," *Annals of the American Academy of Political and Social Science* 66 (2004): 75–79; Hewlett, Sherbin, and Forster, "Off-Ramps and On-Ramps Revisited"; Hewlett et al., *Off-Ramps and On-Ramps Revisited*.

3. P. Stone, *Opting Out? Why Women Really Quit Careers and Head Home* (Berkeley and Los Angeles: University of California Press, 2007).

4. S. A. Hewlett and C. L. Buck, "Off-Ramps and On-Ramps: Keeping Talented Women on the Road to Success," *Harvard Business Review*, March 2005.

5. A. Crittenden, *The Price of Motherhood: Why the Most Important Job in the World Is Still the Least Valued* (New York: Metropolitan Books, 2001).

6. D. Kahneman, *Thinking, Fast and Slow* (New York: Macmillan, 2011).

7. Weisshaar, "From Opt Out to Blocked Out."

8. K. Weisshaar, "Stay-at-Home Moms Are Half as Likely to Get a Job Interview as Moms Who Got Laid Off," hbr.org, February 22, 2018, https://hbr.org/2018/02/stay-at-home-moms-are-half-as-likely-to-get-a-job-interview-as-moms-who-got-laid-off.

9. P. Stone, *Opting Out?*

10. Hewlett and Buck, "Off-Ramps and On-Ramps."

11. J. Brines, "Economic Dependency, Gender, and the Division of Labor at Home," *American Journal of Sociology* 100, no. 3 (1994): 652–688.

12. S. Meers and J. Strober, *Getting to 50/50: How Working Parents Can Have It All* (Jersey City, NJ: Viva Editions, 2013); and S. Sandberg, *Lean In: Women, Work and the Will to Lead* (London: W.H. Allen, 2013).

13. Pew Research Center, *Raising Kids and Running a Household: How Working Parents Share the Load*," Social and Demographic Trends, 2015, http://www.pewsocialtrends.org/2015/11/04/raising-kids-and-running-a-household-how-working-parents-share-the-load/.

14. Office for National Statistics, *Women Shoulder the Responsibility of "Unpaid Work,"* Employment and Labour Market Report, United Kingdom, 2016, https://www.ons.gov.uk/employmentandlabourmarket/peopleinwork/earningsandworkinghours/articles/womenshouldertheresponsibilityofunpaidwork/2016-11-10.

15. T. Dufu, *Drop the Ball: Achieving More by Doing Less* (New York: Flatiron Books, 2017).

Chapter 4

1. I. Padavic, R. Ely, and E. Reid, "Explaining the Persistence of Gender Inequality: The Work-Family Narrative as a Social Defense against the 24/7 Work Culture," *Administrative Science Quarterly* (forthcoming).

2. S. Iyengar, *The Art of Choosing* (Boston: Little, Brown, 2010).

3. G. Ramey and V. A. Ramey, *The Rug Rat Race* (Cambridge, MA: National Bureau of Economic Research, 2009).

4. The NICHD Early Child Care Research Network, ed., *Child Care and Child Development: Results from the NICHD Study of Early Child Care and Youth Development* (New York: Guilford, 2005).

5. J. Bowlby, *A Secure Base: Clinical Applications of Attachment Theory* (Abington, UK: Routledge, 1988).

Chapter 5

1. C. G. Jung, *The Collected Works*, vol. 6, *Psychological Types* (London: Routledge and Kegan Paul, 1971).

2. A. Van Gennep, *Les rites de passage* (1909; Paris: Émile Nourry, 1964); V. Turner, "Betwixt and Between: The Liminal Period in Rites of Passage," *Proceedings of the American Ethnological Society*, Symposium on New Approaches to the Study of Religion (1967): 4–20.

3. H. Ibarra and O. Obodaru, "Betwixt and Between Identities: Liminal Experience in Contemporary Careers," *Research in Organizational Behavior* 35 (2016): 47–64.

Notes

4. W. Bridges, *Transitions: Making Sense of Life's Changes*, 2nd ed. (Cambridge, MA: Da Capo, 2004), 142.

5. H. Ibarra, *Working Identity: Unconventional Strategies for Reinventing Your Career* (Boston: Harvard Business Press, 2004).

6. US Census Bureau, "Number of Divorced Individuals in the United States in 2016, by Age and Sex," *Statistics Portal*, https://www.statista.com/statistics/687930/number-of-divorced-individuals-by-age-and-sex-us/; United Kingdom Office for National Statistics, "Divorces in England and Wales," 2017, https://www.ons.gov.uk/peoplepopulationandcommunity/birthsdeathsandmarriages/divorce/bulletins/divorcesinenglandandwales/2016; OECD Family Database, "Family Dissolution and Children," 2015, https://www.oecd.org/els/family/SF_3_2_Family_dissolution_children.pdf.

7. C. Dweck, *Mindset: Changing the Way You Think to Fulfil Your Potential* (London: Hachette UK, 2017).

8. C. R. Knee, "Implicit Theories of Relationships: Assessment and Prediction of Romantic Relationship Initiation, Coping, and Longevity," *Journal of Personality and Social Psychology* 74 (1998): 360–370.

9. E. J. Finkel, J. L. Burnette, and L. E. Scissors, "Vengefully Ever After: Destiny Beliefs, State Attachment Anxiety, and Forgiveness," *Journal of Personality and Social Psychology* 92, no. 5 (2007): 871–886.

Chapter 6

1. J. L. Petriglieri and O. Obodaru, "Secure-Base Relationships as Drivers of Professional Identity Development in Dual-Career Couples," *Administrative Science Quarterly* (2018), https://doi.org/10.1177%2F0001839218783174.

2. J. Bowlby, *A Secure Base: Clinical Applications of Attachment Theory* (London: Routledge, 1988), 62.

3. J. Bowlby, *Attachment and Loss*, vol. 1, *Attachment* (1969; repr. London: Hogarth Press/Institute of Psychoanalysis, 1982).

4. E. J. Finkel, *The All-or-Nothing Marriage: How the Best Marriages Work* (New York: Penguin, 2017).

Chapter 7

1. E. Galinksy, *Ask the Children: What America's Children Really Think about Working Parents* (Darby, PA: Diane Publishing Company, 1999).

2. R. Clayton, "Can You Afford to Change Your Career?" *Harvard Business Review* digital article, 2018, https://hbr.org/2018/08/can-you-afford-to-change-your-career.

Notes

3. R. M. Rilke, *Letters to a Young Poet*, trans. M. D. Herter Norton (New York: Vintage Books, 1929), 34.

Chapter 8

1. L. Gratton and A. Scott, *The 100-Year Life: Living and Working in an Age of Longevity* (London and New York: Bloomsbury Business, 2017).

2. J. Oeppen and J. Vaupel, "Broken Limits to Life Expectancy," *Science* 295 (2002): 1029–1031; Gratton and Scott, *The 100-Year Life*.

3. OECD Family Database, "Age of Mothers at Childbirth and Age-Specific Fertility," 2018, OECD Social Policy Division, Directorate of Employment, Labour and Social Affairs, https://www.oecd.org/els/soc/SF_2_3_Age_mothers_childbirth.pdf; and Y. S. Khandwala et al., "The Age of Fathers in the USA Is Rising: An Analysis of 168,867,480 Births from 1972 to 2015," *Human Reproduction* 32, no. 10 (2017): 2110–2116.

4. B. Schwartz et al., "Maximizing Versus Satisficing: Happiness Is a Matter of Choice," *Journal of Personality and Social Psychology* 83, no. 5 (2002): 1178–1197; S. S. Iyengar, R. E. Wells, and B. Schwartz," Doing Better but Feeling Worse," *Psychological Science* 17, no. 2 (2006): 143–150; and A. Roets, B. Schwartz, and Y. Guan, "The Tyranny of Choice: A Cross-Cultural Investigation of Maximizing-Satisficing Effects on Well-Being," *Judgment and Decision Making* 7, no. 6 (2012): 689–704.

5. D. W. Winnicott, *Playing and Reality* (London: Tavistock Publications, 1971).

6. G. Sheehy, *Passages: Predictable Crises of Adult Life* (New York: E.P. Dutton, 1974).

7. E. Finkle, *The All-or-Nothing Marriage: How the Best Marriages Work* (New York: Dutton, 2017).

8. S. M. Drigotas et al., "Close Partner as Sculptor of the Ideal Self: Behavioral Affirmation and the Michelangelo Phenomenon," *Journal of Personality and Social Psychology* 77 (1999): 293–323.

9. A. H. Maslow, "A Theory of Human Motivation," *Psychological Review* 50, no. 4 (1943): 370–396.

10. Renee Stepler, "Led by Baby Boomers, Divorce Rates Climb for America's 50+ Population," Pew Research Center, March 9, 2017, http://www.pewresearch.org/fact-tank/2017/03/09/led-by-baby-boomers-divorce-rates-climb-for-americas-50-population/.

11. D. Bair, *Calling It Quits: Late-Life Divorce and Starting Over* (New York: Random House, 2007).

Notes

12. M. J. Rosenfeld, "Who Wants the Breakup? Gender and Breakup in Heterosexual Couples," in *Social Networks and the Life Course*, ed. D. Alwin, D. Felmlee, and D. Kreager (New York: Springer, 2018), 221–243.

13. A. Wittenberg-Cox, *Late Love: Mating in Maturity* (Carlsbad, CA: Motivational Press, 2018).

Chapter 9

1. H. Ibarra and J. L. Petriglieri, "Identity Work and Play," *Journal of Organizational Change Management* 23, no. 1 (2010): 10–25.

Chapter 10

1. E. Fromm, *The Art of Loving* (New York: Harper & Row, 1956).

2. S. Freud, *Civilization and its Discontents* (1930; repr. New York: W.W. Norton and Company, 1962), 48.

Appendix

1. J. E. Pixley, "Differentiating Careers from Jobs in the Search for Dual-Career Couples," *Sociological Perspectives* 52 (2009): 363–384.

2. R. Rapoport and R. N. Rapoport, *Dual-Career Families Re-examined: New Integrations of Work and Family* (London: M. Robertson, 1976).

3. B. G. Glaser and A. Strauss, *The Discovery of Grounded Theory: Strategies for Qualitative Research* (Chicago: Aldine de Gruyter, 1967).

4. R. Atkinson, *The Life Story Interview* (Thousand Oaks, CA: Sage, 1998)

5. A. Strauss and J. M. Corbin, "Grounded Theory Research: Procedures, Canons, and Evaluative Criteria," *Qualitative Sociology* 63 (1990): 284–297.

INDEX

Index

242

Index

Index

Index

Index

ACKNOWLEDGMENTS

This book would not have been written without the couples who generously let me into their lives and shared their stories with me. While only a small number of their stories made it into this book, I learned an immense amount from every couple I spoke to and am deeply appreciative of everything they taught me. Although I cannot name them individually for confidentiality reasons, they know who they are.

Gianpiero was my inspiration for embarking on this project and my constant supporter, sounding board, and muse throughout. He encouraged me through the lows, celebrated with me during the highs, and spent many a late night reading and commenting on the chapters in this book. I am immensely lucky to have him in my life, to be in his life, and to have a life with him and with our children. I am who I am today in good part because of Gianpiero. This book may be the longest love letter I have ever written. It won't be the last.

Our children, Pietro and Arianna, have been unwavering in their excitement for this book. They have debated titles and front covers, encouraged me to make deadlines even when it meant writing during family holidays, and kept me grounded amid the demands of the writing process. They are the sunshine of my life, and now—I promise—we will finish the Magic Allotment books.

Our nanny extraordinaire, Paula Ferriera, keeps our family on track, giving us endless support and care. We are fortunate to have her in our lives.

I am blessed to have many amazing colleagues who have listened to my ideas, challenged my thinking, and encouraged me throughout this process. Otilia Obodaru, with whom I first began researching dual-career couples, helped build the foundations of this work, and I am grateful to have had her as a colleague and friend through its development. Erin Reid and Lakshmi Ramarajan have been particularly supportive in pushing me to write this book and to follow my own path. Many of my colleagues in the Organizational Behavior area at INSEAD have helped along the way, and the school continues to be a fertile ground in which my work can grow. I am especially grateful to Noah Askin, Derek Deasey, Declan Fitzsimons, Spencer Harrison, Sujin Jang, Zoe Kinias, Erin Meyer, and Mette Stuhr. Svenja Weber and Heidi Askin provided invaluable feedback on an early version of some chapters. I am particularly indebted to Herminia Ibarra, who has been, and continues to be, an incredible mentor, role model, supporter, and friend over the years. We met more than a decade ago, and I still feel that I am only beginning to learn all that she has to teach me.

Sarah Green Carmichael, my editor at Harvard Business Review Press, guided me through the process of writing and publishing my first book with enthusiasm and insight. She was an unwavering supporter of my work, and of this work even before I started it, and her love of beautiful writing that makes a difference in people's lives is inspiring and infectious. Lydia Yadi, my editor at Penguin, also contributed enormously to finessing the final manuscript and to guiding me through the publishing process. My wonderful friend and colleague Chris Stephenson-Drake acted as my research assistant, meticulously checking references, reviewing text, and generally keeping me on track. Anna Roberts, a dear friend and fellow writer, has kept me less lonely and more sane over the years of writing. Debbie Egger guided me through the long process of discovering, claiming, and becoming who I am as I wrote this book. Her insight, challenge, and love has kept me in touch with my shadow, and our work together has had a deep influence on my creative work, on these pages and everywhere else.

Friends and family showered me with love and support. I owe a special thanks to my brother Dan and his wife Liz, and to my parents—the first dual-career couple I ever knew—for instilling in me a lifelong curiosity about relationships and work and hinting toward a career in academia as a way to channel my curiosity and as a way of life. My dearest old-time friends, Alison and Paul, continue to be a source of wonder and grace as we age together and keep working on lives and loves worth telling each other about.

ABOUT THE AUTHOR

JENNIFER PETRIGLIERI is an associate professor of Organizational Behavior at INSEAD, an international business school with campuses in France, Singapore, and Abu Dhabi. Her award-winning research and teaching focus on identity, leadership, and career development. She is particularly interested in how people's close relationships shape who they become and how moments of uncertainty and crisis make them who they are.

A British citizen, Jennifer earned a PhD in Organizational Behavior from INSEAD. She also holds an MBA from IMD, Switzerland, and a BSc in genetics from the University of Nottingham, UK. Prior to joining INSEAD, she was a postdoctoral fellow in Organizational Behavior at Harvard Business School. Having lived and worked on three continents, she has now settled in France with her Italian husband, Gianpiero, and their two children. She finds joy in their dual-career life, cooking, pottering in her garden, and spending time in the mountains.